CANYONLANDS NATIONAL PARK AND THE ORGANIC ACT
Balancing Resource Protection and Visitor Use

Foreword

This document is a legal history of the National Park Service's handling of issues related to off-road recreational vehicles in Canyonlands National Park. It was written to provide resource managers with a history of the opinions, discussions, and decisions associated with the balancing of resource protection and visitor use under the 1916 Organic Act.

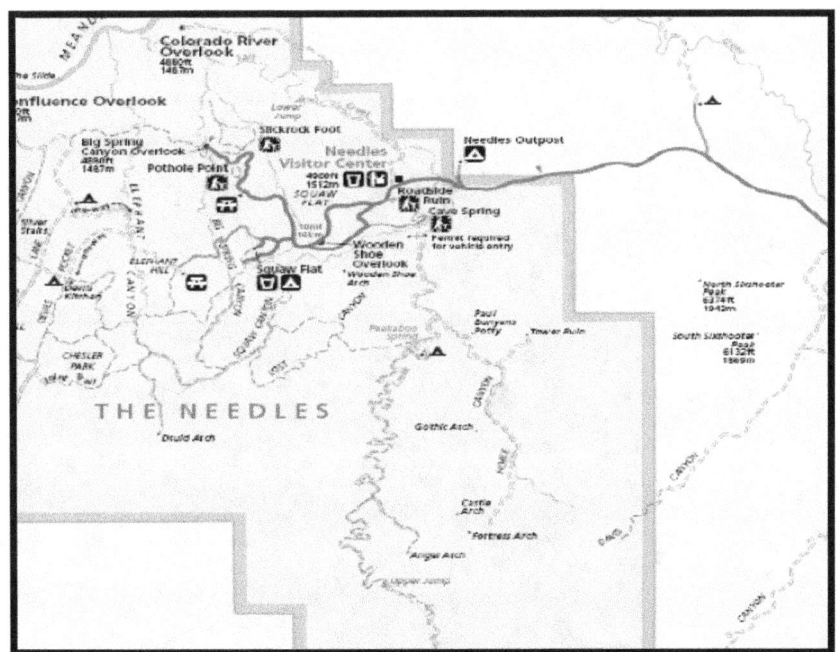

About the Author

Dave Watts is a 1959 graduate of the University of Michigan School of Literature, Science and Arts, and a 1962 graduate of the University of Michigan School of Law. Mr. Watts began working for the Office of the Solicitor in the Department of the Interior in 1963, and in 1970, was named Assistant Solicitor for Parks and Recreation, responsible for the legal work of the National Park Service. As a member of the Senior Executive Service, he was named Deputy Associate Solicitor for the Division of Conservation and Wildlife in 1990, and the Special Assistant to the Solicitor, John Leshy, in 2000. From the days of Interior Secretary Stewart Udall until Mr. Watts' retirement in 2001, he was directly involved in providing legal advice and counsel on the broad array of legal issues impacting the National Park Service.

CANYONLANDS NATIONAL PARK AND THE ORGANIC ACT
Balancing Resource Protection and Visitor Use

CONTENTS

INTRODUCTION

In 1964, President Lyndon B. Johnson signed legislation establishing Canyonlands National Park, which resulted in the transfer of a pristine area of high desert in southeastern Utah from the Bureau of Land Management (BLM) to the National Park Service (NPS). The transfer was more than a symbolic shift in agency control. Management of the 527 square-mile area went from BLM's[1] multiple-use approach to NPS's focused management regime under the 1916 Organic Act [16 U.S.C. §§ 1, 2-4][2] as supplemented by various laws of Congress.

After the transfer, NPS initiated the effort to conform the administration of Canyonlands National Park (Canyonlands) to NPS policies, programs, and regulations. Initially, NPS had to address the serious resource damage resulting from unrestricted, and in some places excessive, public use of the park's backcountry, roads, and trails. These problems had to be resolved to fulfill the mandate of the 1916 Organic Act. One of the troublesome issues was the use of off-road recreational vehicles (ORVs), which increased significantly in the late 1980s with new designs in all-terrain vehicles including oversized tires and high ground clearances. By the 1990s, ORV use could no longer be ignored because over 200 miles of trails were used regularly without limitations. From the NPS perspective, ORV use of the trails appeared to be an invasion. However, many local residents and park visitors viewed this use of the trails as a preexisting right and expected that, without a vigorous public debate, the established patterns and modes of use would continue.

---

[1] The transfer occurred before the passage of the Federal Land Policy and Management Act of 1976 [43 U.S.C.§ 1701]. In 1964, the area was managed under a collage of public land laws, such as the Taylor Grazing Act, Mining Law of 1866, and various oil and gas leasing laws.

[2] Citations to laws will use only United States Code (U.S.C.) notation rather than the more rigorous citation requirements of the Harvard Bluebook. For example, 16 U.S.C. §1 refers to Section 1 of Title 16 of the United States Code. All laws or sections of laws may be found at www.gpoaccess.gov/uscode. The Canyonlands legislation may be found at 16 U.S.C. § 271.

NPS initiated the debate in 1992 by proposing a Backcountry Management Plan (BMP),[3] which was published in 1995. Because the planning effort required compliance with the National Environmental Policy Act (NEPA) [42 U.S.C. § 4332], NPS prepared an Environmental Assessment (EA). The BMP and the EA provided the platform for the public discourse.

The State of Utah and San Juan County also joined the debate, as they asserted ownership and control over the roads and trails within the boundaries of Canyonlands pursuant to a 19th century public land law referred to as R.S. 2477.[4] And, not surprisingly, various environmental organizations were also interested in this dialogue.

NPS efforts were constrained by the conclusions of the 1972 General Management Plan (GMP) for Canyonlands, which had been developed through extensive public debate. Any BMP outside the purview of the GMP could collaterally impeach that GMP or invalidate the BMP, which is, in effect, a subset of the GMP. Significantly, the Canyonlands GMP concluded that Salt Creek Road would remain open to ORVs and noted that NPS had actively maintained that road from Peekaboo Springs to Angel Arch. In addressing ORV uses, the Canyonlands Superintendent had to be careful not to reopen, directly or indirectly, any debate over a resource friendly GMP.

The EA, which was released in December 1993, proposed a plan for controlling ORV use in environmentally sensitive areas. The plan was modest. Because over 200 miles of trails were used predominately by four-wheel-drive vehicles (including ORVs), the EA proposed a permit system to regulate the number of ORVs and their areas of use. In an effort to achieve a balance, the Superintendent decided not to significantly reduce the number of trail miles available for visitor use. However, he stipulated that 24 vehicles per day would be allowed in the Salt Creek and Horse canyon areas, and only 10 per day would be allowed in Lavender Canyon. In addition, the Superintendent stipulated that Davis Canyon would be closed to visitors at the park boundary.

These restrictions were not well received by local recreational users. Consequently, the Superintendent relented and, to accommodate local interests, opened 10 miles of Salt Creek Canyon from Peekaboo Springs to Angle Arch to four-wheel-drive vehicles[5]

---

[3] The BMP can found at www.nps.gov/cany/parkmgmt/upload/backplan.pdf.

[4] R.S. 2477, a law passed in 1866, provided for the appropriation of unreserved public lands by states and counties if the lands were used for public highway purposes. This law was repealed in 1976 by the FLPMA. See 43 U.S.C. § 1769(a). Utah and its counties made broad claims to trails and undeveloped roads in the state within several areas of the National Park System. The contours of these legal claims are well set forth in the Burr Trial litigation. See Sierra Club v. Hodel, 848 F.2d 1068 (10th Cir., 1988) and Sierra Club v. Lujan, 949 F.2d 362 (10th Cir., 1991).

[5] There is a Machiavellian interpretation to the Superintendent's decision to open Salt Creek Canyon: Avoid "heat" from the Utah congressional delegation that would result from closing the road but, instead, let the district court close the road. Ample evidence already existed in the record that ORV use was injurious to park resources, and environmental groups had clearly stated their intention to sue.

(including ORVs) though this approach is not proposed in the EA. (Importantly, Salt Creek is the only year-round water source in the Canyonlands other than the Green and Colorado rivers.) This decision became an Achilles heel, however, as the BMP was challenged by the Southern Utah Wilderness Alliance (SUWA) as part of an overall challenge to the permitting system, NEPA compliance, and protection of park resources under the Organic Act. Not to be left out, the ORV users intervened in the lawsuit, arguing that the NPS went too far in regulating off-road uses. And, in 2001 the State of Utah and San Juan County formally joined as parties because of their R.S. 2477 claims.

The district court sustained the EA analysis as well as the overall BMP, but reversed the Superintendent's decision to keep the 10 miles of the Salt Creek Canyon open to four-wheel-drive vehicles (ORVs). [SUWA v. Dabney, 7 F. Supp 2d 1205 (D.C. Utah 1998)] The court held that the BMP did not honor the NPS's responsibilities under the Organic Act. The case was appealed to the 10th Circuit Court of Appeals by SUWA and the various ORV users, who took opposite sides in the debate. Both argued that the district court erred in sustaining the Canyonlands BMP. The United States did not appeal, because NPS was willing to accept this apparent loss and redo the plan.

During the appeal to the 10th Circuit by SUWA, the United States changed legal positions, arguing that the Superintendent may not have complied with the strictures of the Organic Act and NPS management policies,[6] and that the case should be remanded to the NPS for reconsideration. The court of appeals sustained the new position of the United States and remanded the case to the NPS for compliance with its policies and laws. [SUWA v. Dabney, 222 F.3d 819 (10th Cir 2000)][7]

This litigation was, in essence, a challenge to the NPS's legal roots, involving the proper interpretation of the core legal mandates of the 1916 Organic Act. The remand of the case by the court of appeals with direction to NPS to "get it right" also triggered a comprehensive review by the Clinton Administration of NPS management policies, a review that carried over into the second term of the Bush Administration. For the first time in decades, Congress considered amending the Organic Act. It was not until August 2006 that the debate concluded, at least on the public record. All this activity was the result of a seemingly modest, and arguably balanced, decision to keep open just 10 miles of a popular off-road trail.

However, this interpretation is incorrect. Then Superintendent Dabney advised that the Utah delegation adopted a laissez faire approach and did not apply any political pressure. His decisions were based on resource values and NPS policy.

[6] The latest version of NPS management policies, *Management Policies 2006*, can be found at www.nps.gov/policy/MP2006.pdf.

[7] Web pages on this case may be found through an Internet search of "Southern Utah Wilderness Alliance v. Walt Dabney." Many of the cases cited in this article can be found in this manner. Similarly, one can do a search on the name of the federal court (e.g. Court of Appeals for the 10th Circuit, District Court for the District of Columbia) and find the case by name or date.

The BMP and the ensuing litigation provide an example of unintended consequences. The fundamental issue in this case concerns how to balance conserving park resources with providing for visitor enjoyment. The Organic Act addresses this dichotomy with the requirement "<u>to conserve</u> the scenery and the natural and historic objects and the wild life therein <u>and to provide for the enjoyment</u> of the same in such manner and by such means as will leave them <u>unimpaired</u> for the enjoyment of future generations." [16 U.S.C.§1] (Emphasis added.)

THE BACKCOUNTRY MANAGEMENT PLAN

NPS was forced to address ORV use of Canyonlands as a result of changes in technology, and consequently, in visitor behavior. Instead of enjoying the wonders of the park through backcountry hiking and horseback trips, visitors increasingly used motorized vehicles. Oversized tires and high-lift chassis replaced the hiking boot and horse. Areas of Canyonlands previously accessible to only the young and healthy could now be visited by a many more visitors.

The thesis is simple: Superintendents must be aware of the challenges and dangers of litigation, which takes the debate out of the direct control of the NPS and places the ultimate decision in the hands of the federal court system. The arguments made to the federal courts are, in the final analysis, developed and articulated by the Department of Justice, not the NPS. Consequently, the simplest decisions can result in a serious attack on NPS legal mandates.

There was, however, a significant trade off•serious adverse impacts to the fragile, high-desert ecology. And NPS was forced to address this issue in its management of the area if it wished to comply with its legal mandates and policies. Taking a "pass" on this controversial issue was not an option.

Failure to act could eventually result in another lawsuit.[8] In the 1970s, Redwood National Park was suffering major damage from upstream timber cutting. Because NPS was hamstrung by lack of funds and legal authorities to enjoin the timbering activities, it took no action to acquire the timber lands or abate ongoing injuries. The Sierra Club sued to force the administration to address the problems. In <u>Sierra Club v. Interior</u> [376 F.Supp 90 (DC Calif, 1974)], the district court concluded:

---

[8] The Redwood cases are the seminal litigations regarding failure to act. These cases are part of a collage of litigation standing for the legal principle that NPS has an affirmative duty to act when resources are being impaired; and in these circumstances the courts will grant affirmative relief forcing appropriate action.

Good sense suggests that the existence, nature and extent of potentially damaging conditions on neighboring lands and the effect thereof on the park, and the need for action to prevent such damage are matters that rest, primarily at least, within the judgment of the Secretary. However, <u>neither the terms nor the legislative history of the Redwood National Park Act are such as to preclude judicial review of the Secretary's action or inaction</u>. (Emphasis added.) At 94.

We are of the opinion that the terms of the statute, especially §79c(e), authorizing the Secretary 'in order to afford as full protection as is reasonably possible to the timber, soil, and streams within the boundaries of the park'—'to acquire interests in land from, and to enter into contracts and cooperative agreements with, the owners of land on the periphery of the park and on the watersheds tributary to streams within the park'-- impose a legal duty on the Secretary to utilize the specific powers given to him whenever reasonably necessary for the protection of the park and that any discretion vested in the Secretary concerning time, place and specifics of the exercise of such powers is subordinate to his <u>paramount legal duty imposed, not only under his trust obligation but by the statute itself, to protect the park.</u> At 95. (Emphasis added.)

The litigation continued because the Sierra Club was not satisfied with the NPS's efforts to protect the park from upstream logging. In the next proceeding [<u>Sierra Club v. Interior</u>, 398 F.Supp 284 (DC Calif, 1975)], the district court further illuminated the duty to act when resources are threatened.

As stated in this court's previous opinion the issue for decision is whether the Secretary, since the establishment of the Park, has taken reasonable steps to protect the resources of the Park and, if not, whether his failure to do so has been under the circumstances arbitrary, capricious, or an abuse of discretion.... His acts are presumptively reasonable and in accordance with law and are subject to judicial intervention only when the executive conduct fails to accord with law or is otherwise arbitrary or an abuse of discretion.

With all due respect for the narrow limits of judicial intervention in matters entrusted primarily to executive agencies, the Court concludes that, in light of the foregoing findings, the defendants unreasonably, arbitrarily and in abuse of discretion have failed, refused and neglected to take steps to exercise and perform duties imposed upon them by the National Park System Act, 16 U.S.C. § 1, and the Redwood National Park Act, 16 U.S.C. § 79a, and duties otherwise imposed upon them by law; and/or that defendants have unreasonably and unlawfully delayed taking such steps. (Emphasis added.) At 293.

In the final round of this litigation, Sierra Club v. Interior [424 F.Supp 172 (DC Calif, 1976)], the court defined the outer boundary of the NPS's duty to act to protect park resources.

From the foregoing record and report the court finds and concludes, as has been admitted by plaintiff herein, that the Department of the Interior has now in good faith and to the best of its ability attempted to exercise those powers and to perform those duties as far as possible within the limits of powers and funds provided by the Congress.

The court further finds that, in order adequately to exercise its powers and perform its duties in a manner adequately to protect the Park, Interior now stands in need of new Congressional legislation and/or new Congressional appropriations. (Emphasis added.)

It follows that primary responsibility for the protection of the Park rests, no longer upon Interior, but squarely upon Congress to decide whether and, if so, when, how and to what extent new legislation should be passed to provide additional regulatory powers or funds for protection of the Redwood National Park.

To a lesser extent some responsibility rests upon the Executive, acting through the President's Office of Management and Budget, to decide whether and to what extent it will make recommendations to the Congress for such new legislation and/or additional funds; also it is up to the

Executive to decide whether litigation should be commenced through the Department of Justice against the timber owners. Such recommendations are obviously desirable but they are not matters mandated by existing law.

Such decisions of the Congress and/or the Executive concerning further, future, additional legislation, funds or litigation, involve new policy-making which is the exclusive function of the Congress and the Executive under the doctrine of separation of powers.

For the foregoing reasons, Interior (i.e., the named defendants in this action) is hereby purged of its previously found failure to take steps to exercise and perform duties imposed by 16 U.S.C. s 1 et seq., and 16 U.S.C. s 79a, et seq., (as found in an order of July 16, 1975), and is hereby discharged from further obligation to comply with or further report upon our directives in that order, insofar as such compliance or reporting involves new, additional legislation, funds or litigation. At 175 - 176

In the SUWA case, NPS addressed affirmatively the ORV use. The opinion of the district court in SUWA sets out the history of the planning process, as follows:

The Park Service determined to develop and implement the BMP to address dramatic increases in the numbers of people visiting the area. Work began in the summer of 1992. In the scoping phase, the Park Service identified the problems and issues to be addressed in the BMP, actively soliciting public input through a variety of means, including publication of a Notice of Intent to Prepare the BMP in the Federal Register.

Thirty-eight issues were identified in this phase, including impacts from aircraft overflights, rock climbing, bicycles, saddle and pack stock, and vehicles. Much discussion arose over the balance to be struck between public demand for vehicular access and public demand for preservation of the riparian and cultural resources in Salt Creek and Horse Canyons. At 1207-8.

The district court went on to describe the NEPA compliance as follows:

Between February 1993 and December 1993, a committee of park employees developed a draft plan or environmental assessment, which was released to the public on December 18th. The draft ("EA") described the Park's current policies, alternatives for change, and the environmental consequences of the alternatives described, including the alternative of taking no action. The EA identified the Park Service's preferred alternative for each problem.

With respect to the trails, <u>the preferred alternative was to close the Salt Creek Canyon to vehicles after a particular landmark, Peekaboo Spring, leaving 10 miles to be traversed by foot before reaching Angel Arch.</u> . . . . Under the preferred alternative, 14.25 miles of unpaved road would be closed, reducing the approximate total in Canyonlands from 194 to 179.25. (Emphasis added.)

The EA also listed alternatives recommended by public comment that were considered but rejected. These included closing all the roads in the planning area, which was rejected as unworkable "due to the popularity of vehicle camping and use," and limiting use by implementation of a permit system, which was rejected as cost prohibitive and overly restrictive.

Over 2000 copies of the draft were distributed to the public. The ensuing review period lasted until March 5, 1994. During that time, the Park Service held numerous public meetings, including meetings with a wide range of special interest groups.

In a briefing statement prepared shortly after the meetings' concluded, the Park Service noted the emergence of major controversy with respect to three proposals--those imposing group size limits, placing restrictions on rock climbing, and closing roads. With respect to the latter, the Park Service noted that "<u>the proposal to close any road has touched a nerve in the four-wheel-drive community.</u>" At 1208. (Emphasis added.)

The district court characterized the final agency decision as follows:

> The final BMP was released on January 6, 1995. The BMP adopts a zoning system, dividing the planning area into 19 zones defined with reference to the fragility and uniqueness of the natural resources located within the zone. Visitor use within each zone is permitted accordingly. The trails in the Canyons were to remain open to vehicle traffic, but access would be limited to those obtaining permits. At 1208.

In sum, it appeared that NPS was proceeding in an orderly fashion to establish an administrative record[9] upon which to make a defensible decision. Yet, keeping Salt Creek Canyon open to ORVs was contrary to the preferred alternative and would eventually become problematic.

---

[9] The administrative record comprises all the documents "relied upon and considered" in reaching the final agency decision. It is critical that this record be comprehensive, understandable, and accurate. The success rate for challenges to NPS decisions under the Administrative Procedures Act correlates directly with the quality of the record. In this regard, the record would also include the GMP goal of keeping the Salt Creek Road open.

LEGAL ROOTS

In establishing Canyonlands National Park, the congressional directive was simple.[10]

> In order to preserve an area in the State of Utah <u>possessing superlative scenic, scientific, and archeologic features for the inspiration, benefit, and use of the public</u>, there is hereby established the Canyonlands National Park which, subject to valid existing rights, shall comprise . . . a total of approximately three hundred and thirty-seven thousand two hundred and fifty-eight acres. [16 U.S.C. § 271] (Emphasis added.)[11]

To ease the impacts of the change in grazing management policies in the transition from BLM to NPS administration, Congress provided assurance to ranchers that this activity would not be immediately disrupted. Rather, the change would be more incremental.

> Where any Federal lands included within the Canyonlands National Park are legally occupied or utilized on the date of approval of this Act . . . , <u>the Secretary of the Interior shall permit the persons holding such grazing privileges to continue in the exercise thereof during the term of the lease, permit, or license, and one period of renewal thereafter.</u> [16 U.S.C. § 271b] (Emphasis added.)

Finally, to ensure that this newly acquired area would be administered in accordance with the laws and policies applicable to the National Park System (System) Congress provided:

> Subject to the provisions of this subchapter, the administration, protection, and development of the Canyonlands National Park, as established pursuant to this subchapter, shall be exercised by the Secretary of the Interior <u>in accordance with the provisions of sections 1, 2, 3, and 4 of this title, as amended and supplemented.</u> [16 U.S.C. §271d] (Emphasis added.)

The legislation said no more. For further guidance on the scope of management discretion and the standards for developing a BMP, the Superintendent turned to the Organic Act, which amplifies and informs the mission of NPS. Congress succinctly stated:

---

[10] Many of the original national parks were established by Congress with generalized language. Only in the last quarter of the 20th century did Congress become slightly more eloquent in stating the purposes and values of each park area.

[11] In 1971, Congress added 80,000 acres to the park.

The service thus established shall promote and regulate the use of the Federal areas known as national parks, monuments, and reservations hereinafter specified, ... by such means and measures as conform to the fundamental purpose of the said parks, monuments, and reservations, which purpose is <u>to conserve the scenery</u> and the natural and historic objects and the wild life therein <u>and to provide for the enjoyment</u> of the same in such manner and by such means as will leave them <u>unimpaired for the enjoyment of future generations.</u> [16 U.S.C. § 1] (Emphasis added.)

Congress was also opaque in this legislative guidance.[12] The Organic Act established in juxtaposition the goals of conserving the natural objects and wildlife for the benefit of future generations, while offering their enjoyment to future generations of the visiting public. Whether the goals of conservation and visitor use are mutually consistent, inconsistent, or hierarchical has plagued the NPS since 1916.

The next major legislative event regarding the legal mandates of the NPS occurred in 1978. Congress was persuaded to address the standards for National Park System management and administration. The General Authorities Act of 1970 was amended by what is commonly referred to as the "Redwood Amendment" because the language was contained in legislation expanding Redwood National Park. [16 U.S.C. § 1a-1]

> Congress declares that the national park system, which began with establishment of Yellowstone National Park in 1872, has since grown to include superlative natural, historic, and recreation areas in every major region of the United States, ... and that it is the purpose of this Act to include all such areas in the System and to clarify the authorities applicable to the System.... The <u>authorization of activities</u> shall be construed and the protection, management, and administration of these areas shall be conducted in light of the high public value and integrity of the National Park System and <u>shall not be exercised in derogation of the values and</u>

---

[12] While general in management direction, the Organic Act has some remarkably specific provisions that arguably run contrary to traditional park management concepts, such as timber cutting, killing of wildlife, and grazing. [The Secretary of the Interior] may also, upon terms and conditions to be fixed by him, <u>sell or dispose of timber</u> in those cases where in his judgment the <u>cutting of such timber</u> is required in order to control the attacks of insects or diseases or otherwise conserve the scenery or the natural or historic objects in any such park, monument, or reservation. He may also provide in his discretion for the <u>destruction of such animals and of such plant life</u> as may be detrimental to the use of any of said parks, monuments, or reservations. No natural, curiosities, wonders, or objects of interest shall be leased, rented, or granted to anyone on such terms as to interfere with free access to them by the public: Provided, however, that the Secretary of the Interior may, under such rules and regulations and on such terms as he may prescribe, <u>grant the privilege to graze livestock within any national park, monument,</u> or reservation herein referred to when in his judgment such use is not detrimental to the primary purpose for which such park, monument, or reservation was created, except that this provision shall not apply to the Yellowstone National Park.... 16 U.S.C. § 3. (Emphasis added.)

purposes for which these various areas have been established, except as may have been or shall be directly and specifically provided by Congress. [16 U.S.C. § 1a-1] (Emphasis added.)

In this legislation Congress addressed National Park System management issues from the negative side of the equation: what *not* to do. The 1978 Act [often called "The Redwood Amendment"] is now the gold standard by which most NPS decisions are measured. To facilitate uniformity in the interpretation and the application of this collage of congressional enactments, the NPS also initiated in 1978 the process of developing comprehensive management guidelines. These guidelines were soon addressed in earnest, as a result of the SUWA litigation.

Congress intended the language of the Redwood Amendment to the General Authorities Act to reiterate the provisions of the Organic Act, not create a substantively different management standard. The Senate committee report stated:

> The Secretary is to afford the highest standard of protection and care to the natural resources within . . . the National Park System. No decision shall compromise these resource values except as Congress may have specifically provided. . . . The Secretary has an absolute duty, which is not to be compromised, to fulfill the mandate of the 1916 Act to take whatever actions and seek whatever relief as will safeguard the units of the national park system.[13]

The House committee report described the Redwood amendment as a "declaration by Congress" that the promotion and regulation of the National Park System are to be consistent with the Organic Act. The House report stated, "The Secretary is to afford the highest duty of protection and care [to parklands].[14]

Subsequent judicial opinions addressed the appropriate interpretation of the Organic Act, as amplified by the 1978 Act. These court cases began to inform NPS on how the courts would address its legal mandate. One of the early cases, for example, clearly established the principle that the 1978 Act did *not* create a "trust" responsibility.[15] The District Court for the District of Columbia in Sierra Club v. Andrus [487 F. Supp. 443 (D DC,1980)], considering whether the NPS had to participate in a western water rights adjudication, rejected the argument that the NPS had a "trust" responsibility to protect park resources. The court reached this conclusion under the following rationale:

---

[13] S. Rep. No. 95-528, 95th Congress, 1st Session at 13-14 (1977)

[14] H. Rep. No.95-581, 95th Congress, 2nd Session at 21. (1978)

[15] This legal nuance is important. In the previously discussed California Redwood cases brought by the Sierra Club, the district court concluded in strong language that NPS had a public trust responsibility to protect park resources from injury or damage. The 1978 amendment was specifically designed during the drafting process at Interior to nullify the "trust" concept and to limit NPS duties to the plain words of the various laws.

To the extent that plaintiff's argument advances the proposition that defendants are charged with "trust" duties distinguishable from their statutory duties, the Court disagrees. Rather, the Court views the statutory duties previously discussed as comprising all the responsibilities which defendants must faithfully discharge.

The legislative history of the 1978 amendment to 16 U.S.C. s 1a-1 makes clear that <u>any distinction between "trust" and "statutory"" responsibilities in the management of the National Park System is unfounded.</u> Moreover, Congress specifically addressed the authority upon which plaintiff relies to support its "trust theory." At 449. (Emphasis added.)

Nineteen years later the District Court for the District of Columbia was given another opportunity to consider the trust argument. In <u>Edmonds Institute v. Babbitt</u> [42 F.Supp. 2d 1 (D.D.C., 1999)], the court opined:

[T]his Court considered a claim similar to this one insofar as plaintiffs invoked the organic acts of both the Park Service and the particular park at issue and also the public trust doctrine. . . . The court also examined plaintiff's trust theory and found that <u>Congress has supplanted any trust obligations by enacting the detailed regulatory system</u> governing national parks. . . . [T]here is no reason to question the holding of Sierra Club v. Andrus in this case. At 17.

The judicial decisions after the 1978 Act also began to inform NPS of its duty to protect park resources as the primary goal of Park System management. These cases are interesting precursors to the SUWA litigation.[16] For example, in <u>Bicycle Trails Council of Marin County v. Babbitt</u> [82 F.3d, 1445 (9th Cir, 1996)], involving NPS restrictions on bicycle use in Golden Gate National Recreation Area, the Court of Appeals for the 9th Circuit said:

By a series of amendments to the National Park Service Organic Act, 16 U.S.C. sections 1 et seq., Congress disapproved of this management by categories scheme and directed that all units of the national parks were to be treated consistently, with resource protection the primary goal, while retaining the flexibility for individual park units to approve particular uses consistent with their specific enabling legislation. Thus, NPS eliminated these management categories from its internal administration in 1978 and

---

[16] For additional court decisions regarding the NPS duty to protect park resources, see also <u>Organized Fishermen of Florida v. Hodel</u>, 775 F.2d 1544 (11th Cir. 1984), sustaining fishing bag limits in Everglades National Park; and <u>National Wildlife Federation v. NPS</u>, 669 F.Supp. 384 (DC Wyo 1987), sustaining the discretion of NPS to develop the Fishing Bridge Campground in Yellowstone NP.

ultimately began promulgating regulations in the 1980's eliminating these categorical distinctions from the Code of Federal Regulations. The elimination of the last regulatory reference to these management categories was one of the objectives articulated by NPS for the rulemaking effecting the 1987 regulation. See 52 Fed. Reg. 10670 (April 2, 1987). At 1449 -1450. Congress clearly intended and mandated that NPS eliminate the distinctions and treat all units as it had been treating those parks that had been expressly within the ambit of the Organic Act, the natural and historic units, with resource protection the overarching concern. 1453 (Emphasis added.)

In National Rifle Association v. Potter [628 F. Supp. 903 (D DC, 1986)], which involved a challenge to NPS regulations prohibiting trapping in Park System areas unless specifically authorized by Congress, the court said:

In the Organic Act Congress speaks of but a single purpose, namely, conservation; and the fact that Congress thereafter saw fit in the various acts creating individual units of the Park System to authorize hunting and/or trapping expressly (or to leave such matters to NPS' discretion) leads to a supposition that it expected that they would not be allowed to take place elsewhere. At 909.

The Secretary and the Park Service have been charged by Congress with the responsibility for achieving the sometimes conflicting goals of preserving the country's natural resources for future generations while ensuring their enjoyment by current users. Notwithstanding his recent predecessors may have permitted hunting and trapping in selected park areas of their choosing, the present Secretary has re-examined the subject in the light of recent amendments to the Organic Act and has concluded that his primary management function with respect to Park wildlife is its preservation unless Congress has declared otherwise. The regulation thus issues rationally from that conclusion, and if relief is to be forthcoming, plaintiff must look to Congress for it, not the courts. At 912. (Emphasis added.)

In Michigan United Conservation Clubs v. Lujan [949 F.2nd, 202 (6th Cir. 1991)], regarding NPS prohibition of trapping in two national lakeshores, the court concluded:

Notwithstanding that the goals of user enjoyment and natural preservation may sometimes conflict, the NPS may rationally conclude, in light of the Organic Act and its amendments, that its primary management function with respect to wildlife is preservation unless Congress has declared otherwise. At 207. (Emphasis added.)

Finally, Solicitor Leshy opined on the scope and application of the 1978 Act in a 1996 Solicitor's Opinion. His opinion addressed the act's application to other programmatic decisions made by the Secretary of the Interior[17]:

> Where the administrative record reflects a credible threat or serious injury to park resources, a Secretarial decision to authorize the activity posing the threat could be deemed arbitrary and capricious under APA review[18] if the Secretary did nothing other than acknowledge the existence of the threat. The 1978 Amendment limits the breath of the Secretarial discretion at least to the point of requiring some attention, beyond awareness, be paid to the threat. Any other conclusion marginalizes that legislation's concern with preserving park values and purposes from derogation. At 26.

Yale Professor Robin Winks in his Denver Law Review article, "The National Park Service Act of 1916: 'A Contradictory Mandate'?" also explores this legal issue in persuasive detail. In a thorough review of the historic Organic Act and subsequent legislation, Professor Winks concludes:

> The National Park Service was enjoined by that act [1916 Act], and the mission placed upon the Service was reinforced by subsequent acts [e.g., the Redwood Amendment], to conserve the scenic, natural, and historic resources, and the wild life found in conjunction with those resources, in the units of the National Park System in such a way as to leave them unimpaired; this mission had and has precedence over providing means of access, if those means impair the resources, however much access may add to the enjoyment of future generations. 74 Denver L. Rev. 575, 623 (1997). (Emphasis added.)

These laws represent the legal roots of the NPS and are the cornerstones of judicial scrutiny of its programs, decisions, and activities. Agencies also go to great lengths to interpret, through guidelines and regulations, their views of the scope and nature of their various legal authorities, both authorizations and proscriptions. Such efforts to set in place the bookends of agency discretion are laudable. There is, however, another goal: Have the courts grant judicial deference to the agency's view of its mission.[19] The courts

---

[17] Opinion of April 16, 1998, "Options Regarding Applications of the Hardrock Mineral Prospecting Permits on Acquired Lands Near a Unit of the National Park System." This opinion also concluded significantly that the admonishments of the 1978 Act apply to only the decisions and actions of the Secretary of the Interior, not to the Executive Branch generally.

[18] As discussed below, the Administrative Procedures Act (APA) provides a basis for persons and organizations to sue NPS for decisions that are arbitrary, capricious, or not in accordance with the law.

[19] For a discussion of judicial deference to agency decisions, read Chevron v. NRDC, 467 U.S. 837 (1987). This case may be found through an Internet search of "Chevron v. Natural Resources Defense Council."

have recognized the authority of agencies to change their policies or their interpretations of ambiguous statutes, but the judicial test is rigorous. A change in policy may only receive "Chevron" deference where a clear explanation is provided and a reasonable basis for the adjustment exists. Semantic smokescreens will not pass judicial muster.

All NPS decisions must be viewed through the lens of this succession of congressional laws and agency guidelines. While the guidelines improve the focus, they also represent an effort to achieve internal consistency in the various programs and activities. Equally important, they are also designed to have the finger of "agency deference" placed on the scales of justice.

With respect to the SUWA litigation, the standard for judicial review was the Administrative Procedures Act. The issue for the court was whether the agency's decision was "arbitrary, capricious, an abuse of discretion, or otherwise not in accordance with law." [5 U.S.C. § 706(2)(A)] Conceptually, the courts looked at three elements: NPS legal authorities, existing regulations and guidelines, and the facts or data. When the facts of the debate fall within the bookends of the legal authorities and existing regulations and guidelines the NPS has a greater chance of prevailing. It follows, that the administrative record in these cases, which is generally the exclusive basis for the judicial review, should be meticulously compiled and maintained in all three subject areas.

EXECUTIVE ORDER

The BMP for Canyonlands also had to address President Richard M. Nixon's executive order (E.O.) regarding ORVs.[20] The order provides the following guidance:

---

[20] E.O. 11644 of February 8, 1972, as amended by E.O. 11989 of May 24, 1977, which set forth a rigorous process by which to address ORV use.

Sec. 3. *Zones of Use.* (a) Each respective agency head shall develop and issue regulations and administrative instructions, within six months of the date of this order, to provide for administrative designation of the specific areas and trails on public lands on which the use of off-road vehicles may be permitted, and areas in which the use of off-road vehicles may not be permitted, and set a date by which such designation of all public lands shall be completed. Those regulations shall direct that the designation of such areas and trails will be based upon the protection of the resources of the public lands, promotion of the safety of all users of those lands, and minimization of conflicts among the various uses of those lands. The regulations shall further require that the designation of such areas and trails shall be in accordance with the following:

(1) Areas and trails shall be located to minimize damage to soil, watershed, vegetation, or other resources of the public lands.

(2) Areas and trails shall be located to minimize harassment of wildlife or significant disruption of wildlife habitats.

Section 1. *Purpose.* It is the purpose of this order to establish policies and provide for procedures that will ensure that the use of off-road vehicles on public lands will be controlled and directed so as to protect the resources of those lands, to promote the safety of all users of those lands, and to minimize conflicts among the various uses of those lands

Sec. 4. *Operating Conditions.* Each respective agency head shall develop and publish, within one year of the date of this order, regulations prescribing operating conditions for off-road vehicles on the public lands. These regulations shall be directed at protecting resource values, preserving public health, safety, and welfare, and minimizing use conflicts.

Sec. 9. *Special Protection of the Public Lands.* (a) Notwithstanding the provisions of Section 3 of this Order, the respective agency head shall, whenever he determines that the <u>use of off-road vehicles will cause or is causing considerable adverse effects</u> on the soil, vegetation, wildlife, wildlife habitat or cultural or historic resources of particular areas or trails of the public lands, <u>immediately close such areas</u> or trails to the type of off-road vehicle causing such effects, until such time as he determines that such adverse effects have been eliminated and that measures have been implemented to prevent future recurrence. (b) Each respective agency head is <u>authorized to adopt the policy</u> that portions of the public lands within his jurisdiction shall <u>be closed to use by off-road vehicles except those areas or trails which are suitable and specifically designated as open to such use pursuant to Section 3 of this Order.</u> (Emphasis added.)

This E.O. has an interesting judicial history. Unlike most E.O.s, it is legally enforceable. Most include a disclaimer clause stating that it is intended for the management of the Executive Branch of the United States and is not intended to create any rights or

---

(3) Areas and trails shall be located to minimize conflicts between off-road vehicle use and other existing or proposed recreational uses of the same or neighboring public lands, and to ensure the compatibility of such uses with existing conditions in populated areas, taking into account noise and other factors.

(4) Areas and trails shall not be located in officially designated Wilderness Areas or Primitive Areas. Areas and trails shall be located in areas of the National Park System, Natural Areas, or National Wildlife Refuges and Game Ranges only if the respective agency head determines that off-road vehicle use in such locations will not adversely affect their natural, aesthetic, or scenic values.

(b) The respective agency head shall ensure adequate opportunity for public participation in the promulgation of such regulations and in the designation of areas and trails under this section. (c) The limitations on off-road vehicle use imposed under this section shall not apply to official use.

benefits.[21] However, this E.O. was intended to further the purposes of NEPA. As the district court concluded in Conservation Law Foundation v. Clark [590 F. Supp. 1467 (DC Mass 1984), affirmed 864 F.2d 954 (1ˢᵗ Cir, 1989)], upholding the NPS's plan to regulate ORV use at Cape Code National Seashore:

> Defendants argue that E.O. 11644 as amended by E.O. 11989 does not have the force and effect of law and cannot be enforced by the plaintiffs. The court concludes to the contrary. Executive orders can constitutionally be invested with the status of law if they have "some basis in an act of Congress," "pursuant to either a statutory mandate or delegation of authority from Congress." At 1477. (Emphasis added and internal citations omitted.)

> Furthermore, E.O. 11644 has been enforced explicitly in one case and implicitly in another. In National Wildlife Fed. v. Morton, 393 F.Supp. 1286 (D.D.C.1975), the court invalidated regulations governing ORV use on public lands promulgated by the Bureau of Land Management, finding them inconsistent with the provisions of the Executive Order. And in American Motorcyclist Assoc. v. Watt, 543 F.Supp. 789 (C.D.Cal.1982), after citing favorably to the Morton decision, the court invalidated ORV route selection criteria contained in a Conservation Area Plan prepared by the BLM, on the ground of inconsistency with the revised regulations that the agency had promulgated following Morton, supra. Although neither court specifically addressed the sufficiency of the statutory foundation, they both were plainly satisfied as to the validity of Executive Order 11644. At 1477.

THE LAWSUIT

In 1998, SUWA filed its lawsuit. The parties were numerous. The case was styled: Southern Utah Wilderness Alliance, a nonprofit corporation, Plaintiff, v. Walt Dabney, in his official capacity as superintendent of Canyonlands National Park; Joseph Alston, in his official capacity as superintendent of Glen National Recreation Area; John Cook in his official capacity as Regional Director; and the

---

[21] For example, review the following executive order language: "This order is not intended to, and does not, create any right or benefit, substantive or procedural, enforceable at law or in equity against the United States, its departments, agencies, or entities, its officers, employees, or agents, or any other person." Executive Order: "Promoting Quality and Efficient Health Care in Federal Government Administered or Sponsored Health Care Programs." This language has great legal significance regarding the *2006 Management Policies.*

National Park Service, Defendants, and The Utah Trail Machine Association; the Blue Ribbon Coalition; the High Desert Multiple Use Coalition; the United Four Wheel Drive Associations of U.S. & Canada; and the Historic Access Recovery Project, Defendant-Interveners.

The district court characterized the challenge as follows:

> Plaintiff alleges the Park Service violated the Administrative Procedure Act ("APA") in implementing the BMP in violation of agency regulations, the National Park Service Act, and the National Environmental Policy Act ("NEPA"), and in adopting the permit system without having a rational basis for doing so. At 1209.

Also included in the claim of noncompliance with the APA was an argument concerning the application of Executive Order 11644.

THE LAWYERS

When an agency is sued, one of the first questions that must be addressed is who will defend the case. All cases against the United States are defended by the Attorney General of the United States or his designee [28 U.S.C. §§ 516, 519]; the defense is not provided by the contract consultant lawyers NPS hires nor by the Solicitor's Office. The Department of Justice attorneys for this case were the lawyers at the U.S. Attorney's Office for Utah. They reviewed the legal theories, decided whether to defend the case (i.e., the "red face test"[22]), and determined how the case would be presented to the court.

Because the defense of litigation against an Executive Branch agency, such as the NPS, rests in the unreviewable discretion of the Attorney General or the U.S. Attorney assigned the case, federal litigators may refuse to defend a particular decision or embrace the litigation with enthusiasm[23]. In this context, it is important to ensure that trial counsel has a full and complete understanding of NPS actions, the rational basis for the

---

[22] The test is whether the Government lawyer can make the argument to the court without being embarrassed.

[23] It should also be noted that the Justice Department has the unreviewable discretion to decide not to defend an agency decision. Although it is rarely done, the Justice Department may simply confess judgment against the United States, settle the case, or agree to an injunction against the proposed agency action. The agency, though objecting vigorously, may simply be "rolled." Anecdotal evidence suggests this happened at Big Cypress National Preserve during the 1980s in a dispute over a permit to authorize geophysical exploration for oil. No NEPA or regulatory compliance had been done, and the proposed area of impact was Florida Panther critical habitat. Though NPS refused to sign the permit, the Assistant Secretary for Fish, Wildlife and Parks did sign the permit. The National Parks Conservation Association (NPCA) sued, and the Justice Department refused to defend the case, resulting in withdrawal of the permit.

decisions, and the production of a cogent administrative record. Failure in these tasks is detrimental to NPS.

In this case the legal team comprised the Regional Solicitor's Office in Salt Lake City and the U.S. Attorney for Utah. Neither the Washington Solicitor's Office nor the Justice Department General Litigation Section of the Environment and Natural Resources Division were involved in how the case was presented to the district court. In fact, the case was off the Washington Office's radar screen until the district court's opinion was issued.

If an agency loses in district court, it does not control whether an appeal will be made to further defend its decisions. That authority rests with the Department of Justice. All the agency may do is recommend, as persuasively as possible, an appeal. The United States may not bring an appeal or participate in an appeal without the approval of the Office of the Solicitor General of the Department of Justice. The Solicitor

General is a presidential appointee whose office argues all cases before the Supreme Court of the United States. Similarly, an appeal must be blessed by the Appellate Section of the Environment and Natural Resources Division, including the approval of the Assistant Attorney General for that Division. Within the Department of the Interior, an appeal cannot be recommended to the Justice Department unless the Solicitor, upon advice and recommendation from the Director of the NPS, supports the appeal.

The goal of this multi-layered review is to ensure that the legal positions adopted by the United States in the various federal courts are consistent with other pending cases as well as the legal policies of the sitting Attorney General. Idiosyncratic notions of what the law "is" or "should be" are weeded out in this process. This review also assures the federal bench that an appeal filed by the United States has been well vetted within the Executive Branch.

THE ARGUMENT BEFORE THE DISTRICT COURT

Because this case was handled by the Office of the United States Attorney for the State of Utah with the assistance from the staff at Canyonlands National Park, those offices crafted the defense of the Canyonlands BMP. In this process several critical decisions were made regarding how to structure the legal defense. The first element was a declaration from the Superintendent setting forth the rationale for the decision and how the decision comports with the Organic Act.

This is how the Superintendent viewed his legal duties:

> NPS has interpreted its organic act to both contemplate and permit development of roads and other facilities to provide for visitor access to,

19

use and enjoyment of the resources of national parks, even though such developments (which in many parks include road systems, visitor's centers, lodges, highly-developed campgrounds, and other facilities at a much more intense level of development than any in Canyonlands) inevitably damage resources in the parks. NPS interprets the act to provide scope for management decisions reasonably balancing the intrusion of such development with the natural environment with the commensurate and often conflicting mandate to "provide for the enjoyment of the same" and does not interpret such development to violate the requirement to leave park resources "unimpaired for the enjoyment of future generations."[24]

The brief of the Unites States follows the same theme. The U.S. Attorneys Office further develops the Superintendent's declaration as supporting a "balancing" interpretation of the Organic Act. Specifically, NPS has the discretion to balance visitor use and enjoyment against natural resource conservation. And, the brief includes only one sentence discussing what would be the heart of the case•the Redwood Amendment.

Plaintiff argues that the BCMP's decision to continue historic vehicle access to Salt Creek ... is a violation of the acts of Congress which created both the Park Service and Canyonlands National Park. A fundamental problem with Plaintiff's position, however, is its failure to recognize that there are two potentially conflicting directives in each of these acts, preservation of park resources and public enjoyment of those resources, which each park must balance in making decisions ....

Thus, the organic acts focus on two potentially competing values, resource preservation and public access; and the Park Service is tasked with balancing those values in each park. Govt brief at 53.

THE DISTRICT COURT DECISION

On June 19, 1998, the district court entered its opinion on the disputed BMP. The first argument addressed by the court[25] was compliance with Executive Order 11644.

---

[24] This is the August 1997 declaration of the Superintendent. It is important to note that the declaration does not address the gold standard, the Redwood Amendment, which admonishes against the derogation of the purposes and values for which a park is established. Readers are encouraged to compare this interpretation with that of Professor Winks (stated above).

[25] A summary of the court's opinion is not included because any summary may fail to express the nuances and logic of the judge's conclusion. As a result, the decision will be recited in greater detail.

Plaintiff first claims the Park Service's decision was not in accordance with Park Service regulations prohibiting the designation of off-road vehicle routes within national parks. Plaintiff's argument is based on Executive Order 11644, 37 Fed. Reg. 2887 (Feb. 9, 1972), which mandates restrictions on off-road vehicles when their use results in environmental damage.

The heart of the controversy here lies in the question of whether the jeep trails in the Canyons are routes designated for off-road vehicle use, which are prohibited in national parks, or park roads, upon which motor vehicles may travel. At 1209.

"Park roads" are not defined in the regulation. Park Service management policies concerning park roads exist, but are not helpful here. A 1988 policy guide states that park roads should be well constructed, but also acknowledges that some existing roads are cultural and recreational resources that should be preserved even though they may not meet current engineering standards.

"Off-road vehicle routes" are not defined either. Defendant-Interveners argue that the trails cannot be such routes because the Park Service has never so designated them. However, the question is whether the trails are subject to Executive Order 11644, which effectively prohibits off-road vehicle use in the absence of such a designation by requiring agency heads to affirmatively designate the locations where off-road vehicles may be used.

The Park Service asserts that the Park Service has never considered the trails to be subject to Executive Order 11644, as "evidenced by the fact that the Park has continued to operate the backcountry four-wheel drive road system largely in its present form since the Park's creation in 1964, without any change in response to either the Executive Order or the regulations." The Park Service argues that this belief constitutes its interpretation of a regulatory scheme entrusted to its administration, and, as such, is entitled to great deference.

Leaving aside this Court's doubts as to whether the Park Service's failure directly to respond to the Order and its implementing regulations can be construed as evidence that the agency considered the Order and determined that it did not apply to the jeep trails in the Canyons, this Court does not find that the interpretation of the regulation to exclude roads providing access and circulation within the Park is plainly erroneous or inconsistent with the Order.

The Order's preamble states that the need for the Order arose because off-road vehicle use was occurring on public lands without agencies ever considering whether such use was consistent with wise land and resource management practices. The record reflects here that vehicle use in the Canyons has been considered. Park Service management policies require park access and circulation systems to be identified in general management plans. The backcountry roads, including the jeep trails in the Canyons, are identified in the Park's 1978 General Management Plan. Moreover, vehicle use in the Canyons was extensively considered in the preparation of the BMP at issue in this lawsuit. At 1210-1211. (Emphasis added.)

The NPS dodged a bullet on this issue. The claim for deference was granted by the court, with some hesitation. The NPS interpretation to avoid the thrust of the executive order was remarkable, but persuasive. Credit clearly goes to the U.S. Attorney's Office for convincing the court.

The court next considered the NEPA claims as follows:

NEPA requires federal agencies to prepare detailed statements of the environmental impacts of any major action they propose to undertake that will significantly affect the human environment. See 42 U.S.C. §4332. If an agency is uncertain whether an action will have such an effect, the agency first prepares an EA. See 40 C.F.R. §1501.3. Through the mechanism of the EA, the agency reviews the environmental consequences of a proposed action in sufficient depth to determine whether preparation of the more detailed environmental impact statement ("EIS") is necessary. If the agency finds that the proposed action will not significantly impact the environment (a "FONSI'"), the agency need not prepare an EIS.

Plaintiff argues that the Park Service should have considered a broader range of closure alternatives, ranging from closing all the roads to closing none of the roads, and that the Park Service's decision to consider only alternatives that maximized vehicle use is insupportable in light of the National Park Service Organic Act's directive to "encourage the use of transportation modes other than personal motor vehicles." [16 U.S.C. §2301] At 1212.

This Court cannot say that the range of alternatives considered in the EA prevented an informed discussion, especially in light of the BMP's purpose to address the incremental impact of increased visitation. The Park Service focused on alternatives that were responsive to the problems identified as most critical in the scoping process, and, with respect to those problems, the Park Service did consider a full range of alternatives, including complete closure.

In terms of the perspectives shared and the positions advanced, it is not clear that the debate would have been considerably richer or different if the EA had included the alternative of closing all of the backcountry roads.

Plaintiff next claims that the Park Service violated NEPA and thwarted its primary purpose of subjecting proposed actions to public debate and scrutiny before their final implementation by adopting an alternative that was not presented in the EA. Plaintiff is especially troubled by the Park Service's adoption of an alternative that was explicitly rejected in the EA, as is this Court. At 1213 (Emphasis added.)

Applying these principles in conjunction with the APA's deferential standard of review, this Court cannot conclude that the Park Service's failure to include the permit system as an alternative in the EA violated NEPA. The continued presence of vehicles in the Canyons was contemplated both by the no- action alternative and by several alternatives permitting guided tours. And again, public debate over the alternatives was sufficiently broad to apprise the Park Service of the various public perspectives. At 1214. (Emphasis added.)

The district court's interpretation of NEPA and the CEQ guidelines is encouraging. The court focused on the core issue: a full, public dialogue on a broad array of environmental impacts. On the meaning of the Organic Act's resource protection language, the court concluded:

With respect to Salt Creek Canyon beyond Peekaboo Spring, the first Chevron inquiry is determinative. Congress has issued a clear answer to the question of whether the Park Service is authorized to permit activities within national parks that permanently impair unique park resources. The answer is no. As set out in the statutes discussed above, the Park Service's mandate is to permit forms of enjoyment and access that are consistent with preservation and inconsistent with significant, permanent impairment. (Emphasis added.)

Continued use of vehicles on the Salt Creek Jeep Trial beyond Peekaboo Spring is inconsistent with this clear legislative directive. The administrative record shows both that the riparian areas in Salt Creek Canyon are unique and that the effects of vehicular traffic beyond Peekaboo Spring are inherently and fundamentally inimical to their continued existence. The presence of the jeep trails eliminates areas that would otherwise support rare riparian vegetation and provide a rare habitat for a diverse array of small mammals and birds. Driving vehicles through the water kills aquatic species by increasing turbidity, churning pool bottoms, breaking down banks, and decreasing fish habitat. These

23

are some of the grounds upon which the Park Service defended its selection of closure as the preferred alternative in the initial EA. There is nothing in the administrative record to show that its earlier position was overstated or otherwise in error. At 1211.

With respect to visitor enjoyment provisions of the Organic Act, the court accepted the Government's characterization of the language, an interpretation not universally supported by NPS management.

> The administrative record reflects that the Park Service adopted the permit system instead of the pedestrian-access alternative solely because of the popularity of four-wheel-drive travel. However, "visitor enjoyment" as used in the statute refers to visitor enjoyment of park scenery, wildlife, and natural and historic objects that are to be preserved. As used in this sense, visitor enjoyment does not refer to visitor enjoyment of outdoor recreational activities. Opportunities for outdoor recreation are provided on lands managed by the Bureau of Land Management and the Forest Service. (Emphasis added.)

> Given the uniqueness of its riparian areas and the availability of less-invasive forms of access, permanent impairment of Salt Creek Canyon in order to permit the continued use of four-wheel-drive vehicles beyond Peekaboo Spring cannot be reconciled with the Organic Act's overarching goal of resource protection. At 1212. (Emphasis added.)

Although the NPS "lost" the issue of keeping open the Salt Creek Road, some argued that the court's decision was actually a victory for the preservation of park resources. And further, the standard adopted by the district court clearly tipped the balance of the mandate of visitor enjoyment and resource conservation in favor of the resources. Yet, the definition of visitor enjoyment is, arguably, flawed. The court is basically suggesting that it is simply the scenery and wildlife that are to be enjoyed, not the thrill of driving an ORV, cross-country skiing, or white-water rafting.

Taking a short detour from the decision in the SUWA case, it is worth noting that the NPS has a history of winning when it loses. An example occurred in National Park and Conservation Association v. Stanton [54 F.Supp 2nd 7 (D DC. 1999)], where the district court was asked to address whether NPS could delegate away the management responsibility for the Niobrara National Scenic River [16 U.S.C. § 1274(a)(117)], because NPS was "pressured" into executing a cooperative agreement with local interests that it opposed. The court concluded:

> Recognizing that the area along the River was largely privately-held, Congress limited the amount of land the federal government could acquire, and encouraged state and local involvement in the administration

and management of the River locale. NSRDA, 105 Stat. at 255. Congress also created the eleven member Niobrara Scenic River Advisory Commission ("Advisory Commission"), an advisory group representing local interests, for the purpose of aiding NPS in developing a management plan for the area. At 7. (Emphasis added.)

The Court concludes that Defendant's delegation of its statutory management duties to the Council violates the unlawful delegation doctrine because NPS retains no oversight over the Council, no final reviewing authority over the council's actions or inaction, and the Council's dominant private local interests are likely to conflict with the national environmental interests that NPS is statutorily mandated to represent. The delegation is also unlawful because the Council, made up almost wholly of local commercial and land-owning interests, does not share NPS' national vision and perspective. NPS controls only one of the 15 Council members, and is the only member, besides FWS, who represents national environmental concerns. At 19-20. (Emphasis added.)

To no one's surprise, NPS said "no appeal" to this decision. After all, the court had crafted a remedy that the NPS could not negotiate in the existing political environment. And, although the case was technically a loss in court, it was a great victory for NPS resource management. Likewise, many in NPS believe that the district court made the correct decision in the SUWA case, even though the BMP was rejected in part.

THE SUWA APPEAL

The initial reaction to the decision was to let it lie. However, SUWA forced the issue by lodging an appeal with the Court of Appeals for the 10th Circuit. So, the issue was simply, What should the United States do?

Option one was to do nothing. After all, went the argument, the district court's decision was agreeable to NPS. Because this decision represented just one district court's view of the Organic Act and the opinion emphasized the preservation responsibilities of NPS, it was tempting not to appeal. Closing the Salt Creek Road would actually help protect park resources. And, the NPS could say to the congressional delegation, "the district court made us do that," rather than defend the agency's own decision. The road closure by court order provided effective insulation from political intervention. However, upon reflection, this option was rejected as it became apparent that the United States could not sit on the sidelines during litigation of a legal issue fundamental to the management and administration of the National Park System: The proper interpretation of the Organic Act and the 1978 Redwood Amendment.

25

Option two was to defend the district court's interpretation of the Organic Act. This position had great appeal because the court had clearly placed resource preservation above visitor use when it said, "Congress has issued a clear answer to the question of whether the Park Service is authorized to permit activities within national parks that permanently impair unique park resources. The answer is no."

Option three was to tweak that characterization of the NPS legal mandate with another formulation. After significant internal debate, the NPS Washington Office urged a different interpretation and, equally important, to no longer defend the decision to keep the Salt Creek Road open. Rather, NPS Washington management wanted the case remanded to the Superintendent for application of the modified legal interpretation being developed as an integral part of the management policies. The Justice Department would have to be persuaded to adopt this course of action because it is rare for the United States to change its position in a lawsuit. An "about face" in a lawsuit appears inappropriate, casts doubt on the objectivity of the governmental process, and gives the appearance that political pressure may have been applied.

Nevertheless, the Government chose option three. The basic issue came down to a simple question: Could NPS live with the court's view of the Organic Act? The answer was, No!

The Government's brief and the issues on appeal became significant because the Department of Justice, by filing the brief on behalf of the United States, established the interpretation of the Organic Act in the name of the United States, rather than NPS by adopting management policies. A legal position taken by the Justice Department binds the federal agency, and deviations are not permitted except in special circumstances.[26] This point is important. As will be discussed later, efforts to change policies away from positions taken by the United States in the federal courts are difficult. The agency must persuade the Justice Department that the deviation in legal interpretation is appropriate. And, opponents to the change will argue forcefully that change in the United States's position is politically motivated, not legally based. This argument was used successfully in 2005 by opponents of the proposed changes to the Management Policies.

The Justice Department's brief offered this formulation of NPS legal responsibilities, including a case-by-case assessment in each management decision:

> In light of that [SUWA] decision, the Department of the Interior has conducted a substantive reassessment of the proper construction of the Organic Act, which provides the fundamental authority under which the Department, through the National Park Service, manages the National

---

[26] Cite Justice Department regulations regarding the binding nature of its legal positions.

Park System. On the basis of the reassessment, it is the Department's view that the governing standard, which best comports with the language of the Act, provides that the permanent impairment of those resources whose conservation is essential to the fundamental purposes and values for which an individual park has been established is not permitted under the Organic Act. In turn, the <u>Service has the discretion under the Act to determine what resources are essential to the values and purposes of a particular national park, and what constitutes the permanent impairment of those resources.</u>[27] (Emphasis added.) At 4.

The "bright line" of resource protection articulated by the district court is rejected. Instead a more measured balancing approach is offered as the proper interpretation. Further, the Government's brief rejects the district court's use of "unique" resources because that word is not found in the Organic Act. The brief then goes to note that the NPS policies are now under reconsideration.

[T]he Department believes that the resources whose impairment are addressed by the Act are those whose conservation is essential to those fundamental purposes and values, and that the Act precludes permanent impairment of those resources. In turn, the Department is taking steps to revise park policy consistent with that construction. Brief at 19.

In sum, the Organic Act accords the Service substantial discretion to manage park resources. That discretion allows the Service to assess what are the essential resources of a particular park and what would permanently impair those resources. In turn, while the Organic Act grants the Service broad discretion to manage park resources, the Act also sets the bounds of that discretion. Where the Service finds, as supported by the administrative record, that a particular use would permanently impair an essential resource of a particular park, the Service must manage the park for the lasting benefit of the identified resource. Brief at 24-25.[28]

With respect to visitor enjoyment, the Government argued:

First, while Section 1 [of the Organic Act] does refer to enjoyment of scenery, wildlife and natural and historic objects, the court's differentiation of those forms of enjoyment of outdoor recreation is a false one. Visitors who engage in outdoor recreation in the national parks often do so specifically because of the scenic or other opportunities which a

---

[27] Brief of Federal Appellees, pp 4-5.

[28] Credit is given to Ed Kneedler of the Solicitor General's Office and John Stahr of the Appellate Section of the DENR for carefully crafting the Government's position. The brief was written in a collegial spirit and with a full command of the nuances of the English language and the law.

particular park provides. Indeed, enjoyment of scenery, wildlife, and natural and historic objects, is outdoor recreation. . . . A visitor who is enjoying outdoor recreational opportunities within a park may also simultaneously be enjoying other attractions of the park was well. At 26. (Emphasis in the original.)

THE APPELLATE COURT DECISION

The case was argued by John Stahr, a lawyer from the Appellate Section of the Environment and Natural Resources Division, rather the United States Attorney for the State of Utah. This is generally how high-profile cases are argued on appeal.

The NPS faired well on the appeal.[29]

> Interestingly, the federal defendants did not appeal the district court's decision; however, they did submit a brief to this court "to advise the Court of the Department's views as to the proper legal construction of the [Organic] Act." In that brief, they take a position different from the position taken in the district court. At 822.

> We first note that the district court erred in its framing of the question at issue for purposes of Chevron analysis. The district court characterized the question as whether the NPS is authorized to permit activities within national parks that permanently impair unique park resources. See Southern Utah Wilderness Alliance, 7 F. Supp. 2d at 1211. Stating the question that way predetermines the answer. We believe the precise question at issue is whether the BMP, in particular the portion of the BMP allowing vehicle use on the ten-mile segment of the Salt Creek Road from Peekaboo Spring to Angel Arch, is inconsistent with a clear intent of Congress expressed in the Organic Act and the Canyonlands enabling legislation. Framing the question in terms of "permanent impairment" might not necessarily be erroneous if the administrative record clearly showed that such permanent impairment would occur; however, we find that the record is not clear on that issue. See discussion infra. At 826. (Emphasis added.)

> The Organic Act mandates that the NPS provide for the conservation and enjoyment of the scenery and natural historic objects and the wildlife[30]

---

[29] Rather than lose the nuances of this important case, the decision is quoted at length. The case is found at 222 F.3rd 819. Language from this citation, rather than the slip opinion, is included.

[30] In the original text of the Organic Act, "wildlife" is two words, i.e., "wild life."

therein "in such manner and by such means as will leave them unimpaired for the enjoyment of future generations." 16 U.S.C. § 1 (emphasis added). Neither the word "unimpaired" nor the phrase "unimpaired for the enjoyment of future generations" is defined in the Act. It is unclear from the statute itself what constitutes impairment, and how both the duration and severity of the impairment are to be evaluated or weighed against the other value of public use of the park. At 826.

In its brief to this court and at oral argument, the NPS has advised us that the Department of the Interior "has conducted a substantive reassessment of the proper construction of the Organic Act." On the basis of that reassessment, the Department took the position in its brief to this court that the Act prohibits "permanent impairment of those resources whose conservation is essential to the fundamental purposes and values for which an individual park has been established." The Department also took the position that the NPS has discretion under the Act to determine what resources are essential to the values and purposes of a particular national park, and what constitutes the impairment of those resources. (Emphasis added.)

The Draft Policies propose to define "impairment of park resources and values" as "an adverse impact on one or more park resources or values that interferes with the integrity of the park's resources or values, or with the opportunities that otherwise would exist for the enjoyment of them by a present or future generation." Id. The Draft Policies also propose to define "park resources and values" as "all the resources and values of a park whose conservation is essential to the purposes for which the area was included in the national park system . . . and any additional purposes stated in a park's establishing legislation or proclamation."

The interpretation of the Act now offered by the Department and the NPS in this court and in the Draft Policies varies from the interpretation previously offered by the NPS in the district court. We must determine what weight to give the new interpretation. We conclude that there is currently no valid agency position worthy of deference. At 827.

If the Draft Policies are finalized and adopted pursuant to the requisite rulemaking procedures, and then construed as substantive or legislative rules, they should be accorded Chevron deference; however, if, when ultimately finalized, they lack the requisite formality and are construed merely as interpretative rules, they should be examined under a less deferential standard that asks whether the agency's interpretation is "well reasoned" and "has the power to persuade." At 828.

Moreover, by the time of trial, the Department of the Interior may have finalized and adopted its new NPS Management Policies. <u>If the district court determines that those policies have been expressed in a binding format through the agency's congressionally delegated power, they should be considered legislative rules worthy of Chevron deference. If, however, the district court determines that they are merely interpretative rules, they should be evaluated pursuant to the less deferential standard</u> . . . . At 829. (Emphasis added.)

THE POLICIES

NPS's pilgrimage into administrative guidelines has its own history. To help managers administer the National Park System, in the mid 1960s, separate booklets were prepared on the three primary types of NPS area: natural areas, recreational areas, and historic areas. (The books were green, yellow, and blue, respectively.) This division of management strategies had a legal flaw. Except for the areas established under the Historic Sites Act of 1935[31] [16 U.S.C. § 461], all other areas were established with the Organic Act as their legal foundation. The trilogy of management policies became problematic with the enactment of the 1970 General Authorities Act, which provides:

> [I]t is the purpose of this Act to include all such areas in the System and to clarify the authorities applicable to the system. Congress further reaffirms, declares, and directs that the promotion and regulation of the various areas of the National Park System, as defined in section 2 of this title, shall be consistent with and founded in the purpose established by section 1 of this title, to the common benefit of all the people of the United States. [16 U.S.C. §1-1a]

The effect of this act was to reaffirm the Organic Act as the cornerstone of NPS management. The three books were soon rescinded, and in 1978, NPS began efforts to establish system-wide management policies. As the Court of Appeals for the 9th Circuit noted in the <u>Bicycle Trails of Marin</u> (discussed above):

> By a series of amendments to the National Park Service Organic Act, 16 U.S.C. sections 1 et seq., <u>Congress disapproved of this management by categories scheme</u> and directed that all units of the national parks were to be treated consistently, with resource protection the primary goal, while

---

[31] The Historic Sites Act is a remarkably well crafted law, granting broad authority and discretion to the NPS in management of nationally significant historic resources. The law was very much in vogue from 1950 to 1980. However, late in the 20th Century, it fell into disuse, if not obscurity. Yet, the Historic Sites Act remains an excellent legal tool for managing historic areas of the Park System.

retaining the flexibility for individual park units to approve particular uses consistent with their specific enabling legislation. Thus, NPS eliminated these management categories from its internal administration in 1978 and ultimately began promulgating regulations in the 1980's eliminating these categorical distinctions from the Code of Federal Regulations. The elimination of the last regulatory reference to these management categories was one of the objectives articulated by NPS for the rulemaking effecting the 1987 regulation. See 52 Fed. Reg. 10670 (April 2, 1987). At 1449 -1450. (Emphasis added.)

The revision process was accelerated by the passage of the Paperwork Reduction Act. In the 1990s, the senior managers sought to reduce the volume of administrative guidance and decided to eliminate the four-tier management system. This effort drove the revision of the management policies as well as the effort to make the policies more current. Accordingly, policies and director's orders were introduced.

Returning to the litigation, NPS accepted the challenge and began to finalize the new management guidelines. Some critics of the 2001 management policies have suggested that the whole process was concocted in the waning days of the Clinton Administration, implying a political motive to the exercise. The time-line suggests otherwise:

- In the 1990s, NPS decided to revise its policies and the outmoded four-tier system of directives.

- On June 19, 1998, the district court issued its opinion in the SUWA case.

- On June 30, 1998, NPS published notice in the Federal Register of its intention to revise the policies.

- In May 1999, the Justice Department filed its brief in SUWA case.

- On August 15, 2000, the Court of Appeals for the 10th Circuit reversed the district court and remanded the matter to the NPS.

- On September 15, 2000, NPS published notice in the Federal Register that it had adopted a new policy in section 1.4 on protecting park resources. 65 F.R. 56003.

- In November 2000, the national election was held.

- On November 17, 2000, NPS published Director's Order #55 "Interpreting the National Park Service Organic Act," which superseded Director's Order #55 of September 8, 2000. These orders are, in effect, the precursors to section 1.4 of the 2001 Management Policies.

- On December 27, 2000, the NPS Director declared the new policy in section 1.4 immediately effective.

Yet, time was of the essence — a new administration would arrive in mid-January 2001. NPS finalized the section on park protection in the *2001 Management Policies* just before the change in administration.[32]

More history on the *2001 Management Policies* helps the chronology. In 1986, the Office of the Assistant Secretary for Fish, Wildlife and Parks entered the policy debate over the proper interpretation of the Organic Act. That office floated for public comment a policy that placed visitor use on par with resource conservation. There was one caveat. The visitor use could not permanently or irreparably injure a significant park resource. At issue were the significance of the injury and the time needed to restore the ecosystem.[33] Under this approach, resources within a park could suffer significant degradation as long as NPS could conclude that the injury was reversible over time. The length of time required for resource recovery, however, was never specified in the policy. This proposal created quite an uproar, and the policy initiative was soon abandoned.

NPS issued the controversial section of the 2001 Management Guidelines, after soliciting public comment, to facilitate uniformity in the interpretation and the application of this collage of congressional enactments. Those management policies provided, in part, as follows:

> Congress intended the language of the Redwood amendment to the General Authorities Act to reiterate the provisions of the Organic Act, not create a substantively different management standard. The House committee report described the Redwood amendment as a "declaration by Congress" that the promotion and regulation of the national park system is to be consistent with the Organic Act. The Senate committee report stated that under the Redwood amendment, "The Secretary has an absolute duty, which is not to be compromised, to fulfill the mandate of the 1916 Act to take whatever actions and seek whatever relief as will safeguard the units of the national park system." So, although the Organic Act and the General Authorities Act, as amended by the Redwood amendment, use different wording ("unimpaired" and "derogation")[34] to describe what the

---

[32] The *2001 Management Policies* can be found on the NPS website, www.nps.gov.

[33] This was called the "broken leg policy." The "leg" of a significant resource could be "broken" because it could be repaired over the next 8 months "by using a plaster cast."

[34] This explanation is the effort to logically link the concepts outlined in 1916 Organic Act with the language of the 1978 Redwood Amendment.

National Park Service must avoid, they define a single standard for the management of the national park system—not two different standards. For simplicity, Management Policies uses "impairment," not both statutory phrases, to refer to that single standard. See NPS Management Policies 2001, "'Impairment' and 'Derogation': One Standard" at 1.4.2.

The policies go on to provide a greater level of detail on the theory and philosophy of management.

The "fundamental purpose" of the national park system, established by the Organic Act and reaffirmed by the General Authorities Act, as amended, begins with a mandate to conserve park resources and values. This mandate is independent of the separate prohibition on impairment, and so applies all the time, with respect to all park resources and values, even when there is no risk that any park resources or values may be impaired. NPS managers must always seek ways to avoid, or to minimize to the greatest degree practicable, adverse impacts on park resources and values. However, the <u>laws do give the Service the management discretion to allow impacts to park resources and values when necessary and appropriate to fulfill the purposes of a park, so long as the impact does not constitute impairment of the affected resources and values.</u>

The fundamental purpose of all parks also includes providing for the enjoyment of park resources and values by the people of the United States. <u>The "enjoyment" that is contemplated by the statute is broad; it is the enjoyment of all the people of the United States, not just those who visit parks, and so includes enjoyment both by people who directly experience parks and by those who appreciate them from afar. It also includes deriving benefit (including scientific knowledge) and inspiration from parks, as well as other forms of enjoyment.</u> Congress, recognizing that the enjoyment by future generations of the national parks can be ensured only if the superb quality of park resources and values is left unimpaired, has provided that <u>when there is a conflict between conserving resources and values and providing for enjoyment of them, conservation is to be predominant.</u>[35] This is how courts have consistently interpreted the Organic Act, in decisions that variously describe it as making "resource protection the primary goal" or "resource protection the overarching concern," or as establishing a "primary mission of resource conservation," a "conservation mandate," "an overriding preservation mandate," "an overarching goal of resource protection," or "but a single purpose, namely, conservation." See *NPS Management Policies 2001*, "The NPS Obligation

---

[35] Please note carefully how NPS finessed the conundrum of visitor use vis-à-vis resource protection.

to Conserve and Provide for Enjoyment of Park Resources and Values" at 1.4.3. (Emphasis added.)

Impairment gets the following treatment in the policies from NPS.[36]

> While Congress has given the Service the management discretion to allow certain impacts within parks, that discretion is limited by the statutory requirement (enforceable by the federal courts) that the Park Service must leave park resources and values unimpaired, unless a particular law directly and specifically provides otherwise. This, the cornerstone of the Organic Act, establishes the primary responsibility of the National Park Service. It ensures that park resources and values will continue to exist in a condition that will allow the American people to have present and future opportunities for enjoyment of them. See NPS Management Policies, "The Prohibition on Impairment of Park Resources and Values" at 1.4.4.

In 2004, the Bush administration had a different "take" on what the guidelines should provide. The issue was how to reshape the balance between visitor use and resource protection. The revision effort was again led by the Office of the Assistant Secretary for Fish, Wildlife and Parks, with encouragement from the various ORV use groups and some members of Congress. And, the proposed changes, not surprisingly, reflected the philosophy that political appointees, once invested in office, have the discretion to change agency policies to reflect the views of the current administration.

In October 2005, a revised version of the policies was made available for public review.[37] Editing some of the materials in the 2001 Policies and adding items of questionable relevance[38] gave the Organic Act and the 1978 Redwood Amendment a new twist. The policies refocused the debate on the balance between resource protection and visitor use. Section 1.4.3 of the Policies proposed to include the following:

> The Park Service recognizes that activities in which park visitors engage can cause impacts to park resources and values, and the Service must

---

[36] See *NPS Management Policies 2001*, "The NPS Obligation to Conserve and Provide for Enjoyment of Park Resources and Values," at 1.4.3. See also Special Edition of the Denver Law Review of 1997, volume 74, issue 3. The lawyer's citation is 74 Denver L. Rev. 567 (1997).

[37] The draft policies can be found on the NPCA website, www.npca.org/search with the key words being "management policies." To save paper, the policies are not reprinted in detail because the key issue of visitor use vis-à-vis resource conservation, went through a series of revisions. The Federal Register citation is 70 F.R. 60852.

[38] The draft guidelines also proposed to address items previously considered in the Director's Orders, such as Facilities Management, Business-Like Concession program, Budget Performance and Accountability Programs, Human Capital, Career Development, Succession Planning, Workforce Planning, Employee Safety and Health, and Workforce Diversity.

balance the sometimes competing obligations of conservation and enjoyment in managing the parks. (Emphasis added.)

This language clearly adjusted the balance by placing visitor use on a level of importance comparable with resource protection. In fact, under this standard, visitor use could even "trump" resource protection in the discretion of the NPS. In addition, the new draft replaces "adverse impacts" with the words "unacceptable impacts." Semantics make a significant difference in this matter.

Interestingly, the proposed "balancing" does not fit well with the existing case law previously discussed or with the legal position taken by the Justice Department in the SUWA case. It would appear that the policy folks were willing in 2005 to accept judicial challenges under the amended policies and urge the Justice Department to take another "tack" in any future litigation. After all, the new policies might prevail!

In defense of the policy change, former Assistant Secretary for Fish, Wildlife and Park, William Horn, parsed the legal issue this way at the November 1, 2005, hearing before the National Parks Subcommittee of the Senate Energy and Natural Resources Committee:

> Sound management policies must faithfully track the law, and particular attention needs to be paid to the specific language that Congress adopted nearly a century ago. The mandate is articulated as a single purpose. The language in the statute is "which purpose is." It is not two purposes with one primary and the other subordinate.
>
> Congress also prescribed in 1916 that resources be conserved, not preserved. And last and of critical importance is the express purpose of conserving these resources and leaving them unimpaired. To quote the statute, that is to assure "for the enjoyment of future generations." From a close reading of the statute, it is very evident that public use and enjoyment is inextricably embedded in the single fundamental purpose of our park system, and the 1916 Act, read as a whole, is a mandate for an active management program to facilitate such use and enjoyment.
>
> Now, the only subsequent prescription that arises from the 1916 Act is to assure that park resources are "unimpaired." Now, advocates of public use restrictions invariably define impairment so broadly that many traditional activities can be deemed to cause impairment and therefore be prohibited. For example, the Clinton administration's 2000 rewrite of the NPS policies at section 1.4.5 disturbingly singled out three kinds of activities as sources for impairment: "visitor activities," "NPS activities in the course of managing a park," and "activities undertaken by concessioners, contractors, and others operating in the park."

The disconnect between the Organic Act and the 2001 policies is illustrated by the fact that these specific activities are expressly authorized in sections 1 and 3 of the 1916 Act. Nonetheless, despite their express representation and provision in the 1916 Act, they were tagged as the sources of impairment in the 2001 management policies. In my mind, that is a clear element of disconnect that was worthy of correction.

The Organic Act was enacted with specific contemplation that some resource impacts would attend visitor use and enjoyment. Imagine today trying to build a fraction of Yellowstone's 200-mile loop road system or even one of its historic hotels or lodges. It is an absolute certainty that alleged impairment would be the basis for objections to this form of visitor development. Obviously, Yellowstone's roads and visitor service centers have an impact. Yet, it was decided years ago, consistent with the Organic Act standard, that such impacts were acceptable to facilitate reasonable levels of public use and enjoyment. And I think it is clear that the vast majority of Americans would still agree that the effects of these developments do not constitute an illegal impairment.

Accordingly, the term "impairment" must be defined reasonably and consistently so it does not become a weapon to be used against the use and enjoyment mandate from the basic Organic Act. The definition proposed in the new management policies in my opinion better reflects the law and the need for balance, consistent with the single purpose articulated by Congress in 1916.

The only substantive prescription in the 1916 Act is to assure that park resources are "unimpaired" and definition of this term has become key. Those seeking to restrict public use and enjoyment invariably define "impairment" so broadly that a vast array of traditional park visitor activities can be deemed to cause impairment and, therefore, be prohibited. For example, the Clinton Administration's rewrite of NPS Management Policies stated "AN IMPACT TO ANY PARK RESOURCE OR VALUE may constitute impairment.'" (Caps in original.) NPS Management Policies 2001, 1.4.5.

The same policies go on to provide that an "impact" that simply "affects" a resource or value can also constitute impairment. Id. Lastly, any impact that "would harm the integrity of park resource or values" is proscribed although "integrity" is never defined. . . . <u>Policies that contradict specific Congressional directives are clearly illegal and a rewrite of these misdirected provisions is needed.</u> (Emphasis added.)

The opposite point of view regarding the proposed changes was presented on November 1, 2005, by retired Deputy Director of the National Park Service, Denis Galvin, representing the National Parks and Conservation Association, before the Senate Subcommittee on National Parks.[39] Mr. Galvin was personally and substantially involved in the development of the 2001 Policies. He assessed the proposed changes as follows:

> The fundamental re-interpretation of the Organic Act that is being proposed in the rewrite of the Management Policies does not make it a better document for agency manager's guidance. In fact, the proposed changes would remove the clear guidance of the 2001 edition, and replace it with muddy, unclear, and too-broad discretion left to NPS managers and Administration appointees, to judge what is and is not appropriate use of the national parks. A clear service-wide standard for day-to-day management decision-making is proposed to be replaced with a much broader range of choices.

> There is clearly no need to amend the NPS Organic Act, or any of the other laws governing how our national parks are intended to be managed. The Organic Act has endured soundly for 90 years, and will probably be good for another 90 years, at least.

> Over the 90 years history of the NPS, there has been much debate over whether the NPS is achieving the proper balance between use of the parks for today, and conserving them unimpaired for future generations. These conflicts usually erupt over day-to-day management of particular parks, and the decisions that the NPS makes as it goes through periodic management planning. It is crucial to this discussion, however, to note that there is no credible debate over whether parks should be used by the American people, the debate centers on how the use occurs, or sometimes when or where.

> The interpretation of the NPS Organic Act that is contained in the proposed new version of NPS Management Policies is misguided. It misinterprets the intent of Congress, it ignores numerous federal court decisions, and it greatly weakens the professional judgment of the NPS career managers who have worked under the various NPS laws for over 90 years. Our analysis of key sections of Chapter 1 follows:

---

[39] Rather than include many of the statements before the House and Senate committees or attempt to encapsulate all the diverse views, presented is the testimony of former Deputy Director Galvin, as he was directly involved in drafting the *2001 Management Policies.*

The 2001 Edition further states, "NPS managers must always seek ways to avoid, or to minimize to the greatest extent practicable, adverse impacts on park resources and values." Avoiding adverse impacts is necessitated by both the first element of the single purpose, as well as the second element.

The proposed draft significantly revises the interpretation of the Organic Act by treating its mandate as a balancing act between conservation of resources and values and visitor enjoyment. "The Park Service recognizes that activities in which park visitors engage can cause impacts to park resources and values, and the Service must balance the sometimes competing obligations of conservation and enjoyment in managing the parks."

This interpretation of the Organic Act's fundamental purpose for the NPS is not accurate. While there is clearly a difference between impacts and impairments•NPS may permit certain impacts to park resources and values so long as they are not impairments•the professional judgment that is called for to distinguish between impacts and impairments is clearly different than one that seeks to balance use with conserving . . . unimpaired.

By eliminating the separate Organic Act requirement to conserve park resources and values, the proposed draft relaxes the standards by which a park manager would judge the condition of park resources and values. The draft replaces the phrase "adverse impacts" used in the 2001 edition with the term" unacceptable impacts," a far more indefinite term, that leaves the park manger with little guidance, broad discretion, and an expectation that he or she will "balance" use with conserving . . . unimpaired.

In fact, the park manager does not have "broad discretion" as it is defined in the proposed draft. While federal courts have shown deference to the federal decision-maker in questions about defining impairment, these same courts have universally upheld the paramount mandate of the Organic Act to conserve park resources and values unimpaired, even to the extent of reducing or eliminating a particular form of use.

In his testimony of February 15, 2006, before the House Subcommittee on National Parks, former Deputy Director Galvin addressed in far greater detail the specific concerns over the proposed changes to the 2001 policies.

One of the common explanations provided by Park Service leaders for the proposed changes to management policies is that there is a need to update the 2001 policies to reflect substantive legal changes affecting the agency that have passed into law. For instance, Deputy Director Don Murphy

38

recently stated in the New York Times (1/10/2006) that the proposed management policy changes were needed because "laws have changed, regulations have changed, and times have changed. We have greater responsibilities for homeland security."

We enthusiastically challenge this proposition, which appears to be an argument borne more from a need to justify a flawed process than an argument that has its roots in reality. Since 2001, there have been no amendments to the 1916 Organic Act.

The revisions entirely removes the language referring to the Organic Act as beginning "with a mandate to conserve park resources and values" and that this mandate "is independent of the separate prohibition on impairment, and so applies all the time, with respect to all park resources and values, even when there is no risk that any park resources or values may be impaired." This section also removes the language describing how "Congress recognizing that the enjoyment by future generations of the national parks can be ensured only if the superb quality of park resources and values is left unimpaired, has provided that when there is a conflict between conserving resources and values and providing for enjoyment of them, conservation is to be predominant." Finally this section deletes the explanation that the courts "have consistently interpreted the Organic Act, in decisions that variously describe it as making resource protection the primary goal or resource protection the overarching concern, or as establishing a primary mission of resource conservation, a conservation mandate, an overriding preservation mandate, an overarching goal of resource protection, or but a single purpose, namely, conservation."

> Concern: These revisions reinterpret the NPS Organic Act and reduce the clarity of the NPS mission. The deleted language reflected 80 years of NPS policy that established conservation and resource protection as the NPS primary purpose. The language was replaced with more ambiguous language dispersed throughout the document that, in the aggregate, de-emphasizes the importance of resource protection and might lead some readers to conclude that NPS has a dual purpose, namely protecting resources and providing opportunities for enjoyment, and that the latter is given as much weight as resource protection. If the deleted language were retained, the ambiguity of all the other sections would be removed.

> Specific Revisions: The revision inserts the following guidance, "The Park Service recognizes that activities in

which park visitors engage can cause impacts to park resources and values, and the Service must <u>balance</u> (emphasis added) the sometimes competing obligations of conservation and enjoyment in managing the parks. The courts have recognized that the Service has broad discretion in determining how best to fulfill the Organic Act's mandate."

Concern: The overarching mandate as set down in the Organic Act is to protect park resources. Nowhere in the statutes governing the parks is the NPS instructed to "balance" resource preservation and visitor use. Furthermore, the park manager does not have "broad discretion" as to how to fulfill the Organic Act mandate as stated in the proposed draft. While federal courts have shown deference to the federal decision-maker in questions about defining impairment, these same courts have universally upheld the paramount mandate of the Organic Act to conserve park resources and values unimpaired, even to the extent of reducing or eliminating a particular form of use.

Mr. Galvin's testimony then turned to the issue of visitor use, ORV use in particular, and then to the Executive Order. He observed:

Nevertheless, some want to engage in thrill-type recreation activities, mostly in various types of motorized vehicles, in the national parks. Some (but far from all) park gateway communities complain that they could draw in more tourists if the NPS were "less restrictive" of various uses. These types of demands would seek to kill the goose that lays the golden egg, and must be rejected or ignored.

The national parks do not have to sustain all recreation; that is why we have various other federal, state, local, and private recreation providers to share the demand, and to provide for those types of recreation that generally do not belong in the national parks, or that must be carefully limited. The 1916 NPS Organic Act, emphasizing conservation for future generations, is substantially different from the organic laws of the Bureau of Land Management, the U.S. Forest Service, the U.S. Fish and Wildlife Service, the Army Corps of Engineers, or any other federal agency. The NPS mission is also different from that of state park agencies, or of county or city park agencies. Together, these agencies provide for many forms of public recreation but not all forms of recreation are appropriate in national parks. The snowmobile controversy in Yellowstone would be far less significant if there were no impacts on wintering bison and trumpeter swans.

The off-road vehicle debate at Cape Hatteras would be moderated if there were no impacts on breeding birds, or if more of the beaches were limited to pedestrian use; Section 8.2.3 - Use of Motorized Equipment - Deleted: "Where such use is necessary and appropriate, the least impacting equipment, vehicles, and transportation systems should be used."

> Concern: The snowmobile controversy in Yellowstone is a good example. The National Park Service and the Environmental Protection Agency have independently concluded in three major studies since 2000 that allowing snowmobile use to continue in Yellowstone ... even with limits on the number and type of snowmobiles results in significantly more noise, exhaust, wildlife disturbance, and human health risks than the environmentally-preferred alternative of replacing snowmobiles with snow coaches. The new draft policies remove specific direction to the National Park Service to heed such scientific conclusions and use only the least impacting equipment and vehicles. This opens the door to more snowmobiling and associated noise and air pollution, and wildlife disturbance, not only in Yellowstone but also in other national parks.

8.2.3.1 • Off-road Vehicle Use • Deleted: "Off- road motor vehicle use in national park units is governed by Executive Order 11644 (as amended by Executive Order 11989)...." "Routes and areas may be designated only in locations in which there will be no adverse impacts on the area's natural, cultural, scenic and esthetic values, and in consideration of other visitor uses." "Consistent with the executive orders and the Organic Act, park managers must immediately close a designated off- road vehicle route whenever the use is causing, or will cause, unacceptable adverse effects on the soil, vegetation, wildlife, wildlife habitat, or cultural or historic resources."

> Concern: These combined changes reduce clarity for park managers regarding adverse and unacceptable impacts, and therefore overall management, of off-road vehicles. First, they remove reference to the specific executive order numbers that provide the basis for managing off-road vehicles (and that provide more explicit language on types of unacceptable impacts). In addition to not providing guidance on which executive orders to refer to, the new

policies also remove specific reference to the types of off-road vehicle impacts, including soil, vegetation, wildlife, cultural and visitor impacts, that are unacceptable. How will a park manager use these new policies to determine when and where to actually close routes with no reference to the types of impacts that might justify such closures? If those impacts have been codified anywhere, the new regulations provide no guidance as to where that information can be found. This leaves off-road vehicle impact problems largely up to the discretion of individual park managers.

The story ended after a series of congressional hearings.[40] NPS professionals generally prevailed, and in August 2006, the revised Management Policies were announced with much fanfare. Conceptually, they were much like the 2001 Policies. Sample excerpts in the text boxes below illustrate the similarity.

The Congressional Research Service assessed the process this way in its September 26, 2006, report:

The NPS received approximately 45,000 comments, and made revisions to the draft policies based on these comments. The draft underwent further

---

[40] See S. Hrg 109-313, Part I, Nov 1, 2005. The full testimonies of the Deputy Director and NPS witnesses at the hearings are not presented because they generally reflected the Administration's support for the change, probably at the insistence of OMB and the Assistant Secretary's Office. However, a short excerpt of the testimony is presented to help clarify the matter.

The revision defines and welcomes "appropriate uses" and establishes a clear process by which managers can identify appropriate uses. Appropriate uses are defined as "a use that is suitable, proper or fitting for a particular park, or to a particular location within a park." This definition rests within the broader Park System mission mentioned above: conserving park resources and values while providing for their enjoyment so as to leave them unimpaired for the enjoyment of future generations. The question asked about this revision is "why now?" The answer is simple, yet multi-faceted. The world is changing, and we continue to strive for excellence. Excellence means improving NPS guidance on not only preventing impairment but on preventing "unacceptable impacts" to ensure that impairment will not be reached. Excellence means increasing the understanding of "appropriate use" and ensuring that this component of the fundamental mission is not overlooked. Excellence means keeping the key management decisions in the hands of the managers by better defining "professional judgment."

Another answer to "Why now?" is that the existing management policies do not address "management excellence" and "sustainability" with clarity. NPS faces an evolving context of new technologies, new homeland security challenges, and public demands for efficient and transparent management practices that affect our stewardship responsibilities. NPS must keep pace with these changes. With changing demographics and with the ever-increasing importance of our NPS stewardship, cooperative conservation, civic engagement, and 21st century relevance are critical. One final answer to "Why now?" is that some members of Congress have also expressed an interest in seeing the NPS review its policies. (Emphasis added.) See also House Subcommittee on National Parks oversight hearing on the 2001 policies on April 25, 2002.

review, for example by the National Leadership Council. On June 19, 2006, the NPS issued revised draft management polices. That version was widely viewed as shifting park priorities back to preservation, and was thus generally supported by conservation interests. Some critics viewed the policies as favoring conservation over recreation, and thus as insufficiently allowing for public use and enjoyment of NPS lands and resources. Others viewed the policies as failing to address or resolve certain issues. After a final review and relatively minor revisions, the polices were made final on August 31, 2006.

The final policies contain a list of underlying principles, including that the policies must "ensure that conservation will be predominant when there is a conflict between the protection of resources and their use" (p. iv). In testimony on June 20, 2006, the NPS Deputy Director outlined the "improvement" from the 2001 to 2006 policies, primarily changes in emphasis and clarity in many areas. They include a commitment to civic engagement, cooperative conservation, and improvements in workforce and business practices. Other changes involve additional guidance on relationships between parks and Native Americans, and recognition of the importance of clean air, clean water, and soundscapes. Still other changes involve new guidance on determining what is an appropriate or inappropriate use of parks, and management of uses to avoid impairment of resources. In testimony on July 25, 2006, the NPS Director further elaborated that the 2006 policies ensure that Americans will continue to enjoy national parks. At 9-10.

At the June 20, 2006, Senate Subcommittee hearing, Senator Thomas characterized the conclusion of the process as follows:

This administration has set out to change the management policies in August 2005 and faced some strong public and congressional opposition to the initial draft. Specific concerns were identified in the hearing of the subcommittee last November through public comment that ended in 2006. Many comments focused on the definition of impairing, the definition of impairment and the relationship between the use of the conservation of resources.

The Secretary of the Interior, Gail [sic] Norton, settled the debate on March 17, 2006, in a letter, when she stated that when there is a conflict between the production of resources and use, conservation is predominant.

The adoption of management policies has another goal in addition to seeking deference in judicial review. It is also an expression of the management theory of fostering "consistency" in agency decisionmaking. However, consistency should not be confused with symmetry. What is good for Yellowstone National Park in Wyoming may have only marginal value for Gateway National Recreation Area in New York. That dichotomy should be the real challenge in developing policies.

From a legal perspective, another provision of the 2006 Policies has major legal consequences regarding judicial enforcement.

> The policies contained within this document are intended only to improve the internal management of the National Park Service; <u>they are not intended to, and do not, create any right or benefit, substantive or procedural, enforceable at law or equity by a party against the United States, its departments, agencies, instrumentalities or entities, its officers or employees, or any other person.</u> Park superintendents will be held accountable for their and their staff's, adherence to Service-wide policy. (Emphasis added.)

This language is taken from presidential executive orders in an attempt to disclaim the establishment of any right to litigate noncompliance with the 2006 Policies. This is a major change in approach from the 2001 Policies.[41]

The real issue is whether the 2006 Policies have any "teeth." Historically, the courts have given legal significance to NPS management guidelines, requiring agency compliance. In <u>Davis v. Latschar</u>, 202 F.3d 359 (DC Cir., 2000), the court of appeals reviewed the application of NPS policies regarding the removal of surplus deer at Gettysburg National Military Park and adopted in full the 1998 district court's decision sustaining the deer removal program. The district court said:

> If the Organic Act were the only authority limiting the management discretion of the Park Service, the analysis would end here. But the Park Service has further <u>bound its own discretion through the adoption of Management Policies.</u> (Emphasis added.) At 366.

> The interpretation of the Management Policies proffered by the Park Service is not "plainly erroneous or inconsistent" with the plain terms of the policies and therefore is entitled to deference. At 367.

---

[41] The retention of this provision was noted and objected to by NPCA as follows: "Third Party Enforceability: We objected to the new provision that says that the policies do not create any enforceable benefit by a party in a suit against the United States. This provision remains in the June draft—one change we believe to be unfortunate. However, the policies can still be used as evidence in challenges to laws and regulations." S. Hrg, 109-313, Part II at p 12.

In <u>Voyageurs National Park Ass'n v. Lujan</u> [1991 WL 34770, D.C. Minn, 1991, affirmed at 966 F.2nd 424 (8th Cir. 1992)], the district court recognized that policies may have a waiver provision like that now vested in the Director of the NPS, and that a properly executed waiver will receive deference.

> It appears clear that in general the Department of the Interior has interpreted its statutory obligation under the Wilderness Act as requiring that potential wilderness designation sites be maintained in a pristine state free of motor vehicle traffic, but that this policy has not been implemented with respect to Voyageurs. Indeed, the memorandum announcing the "waiver" of National Park Service policies regarding snowmobiling with respect to the Voyageurs National Park expressly notes that Voyageurs National Park presents a "unique" case justifying departure from <u>otherwise applicable agency policies</u>. (Emphasis added.)

However, the Bush Administration had another view of the binding nature of the 2001 Policies. As previously noted, the 2006 Policies now provide, "They are not intended to, and do not, create any right or benefit, substantive or procedural, enforceable at law or equity by a party against the United States, its departments, agencies, instrumentalities or entities, its officers or employees, or any other person."

It is, therefore, not surprising that the Justice Department and NPS significantly retreated in contemporaneous litigation from the binding nature of the policies and the district court's language in the <u>Gettysburg</u> case.[42] In <u>The Wilderness Society v. Norton</u> [DC Cir, 2006,[43]], the Court of Appeals for the District of Columbia addressed the question of whether NPS had failed to perform its legal duty to report areas suitable for inclusion in the National Wilderness System to the president in a timely manner. [See 16. U.S.C. § 1131.] The court rejected the statutory language argument that reporting was mandated, concluding that the agency had discretion in the timing and manner of its reports.

---

[42] For other cases suggesting that the Management Policies are binding, see <u>Fund for Animals v. Norton</u>, 294 F.Supp, 92, 106 n.8 D.D.C. 2003) holding that NPS policies are binding because "the intent to be bound is clear, as these policies were not simply internal, informal guidelines;" and <u>Sierra Club v. Lujan</u>, 716 F.Supp.1289, 1293 D.C. Ariz. 1989), stating that "NPS must adhere to its Management Policies unless those policies are waived by the Secretary of the Interior . . . or the Director of the Park Service."

[43] This case can be found at www.ll.georgetown.edu/federal/judicial/dc/opinion using January 2006, as the date for location. The page numbers to the materials are from the slip opinion as it appears on the web page.

1.4.3 [2006] The NPS Obligation to Conserve and Provide for Enjoyment of Park Resources and Values. The fundamental purpose of the national park system, established by the Organic Act and reaffirmed by the General Authorities Act, as amended, begins with a mandate to conserve park resources and values. This mandate is independent of the separate prohibition on impairment and applies all the time with respect to all park resources and values, even when there is no risk that any park resources or values may be impaired. NPS managers must always seek ways to avoid, or to minimize to the greatest extent practicable, adverse impacts on park resources and values. However, the laws do give the Service the management discretion to allow impacts to park resources and values when necessary and appropriate to fulfill the purposes of a park, so long as the impact does not constitute impairment of the affected resources and values.

The fundamental purpose of all parks also includes providing for the enjoyment of park resources and values by the people of the United States. The enjoyment that is contemplated by the statute is broad; it is the enjoyment of all the people of the United States and includes enjoyment both by people who visit parks and by those who appreciate them from afar. It also includes deriving benefit (including scientific knowledge) and inspiration from parks, as well as other forms of enjoyment and inspiration. Congress, recognizing that the enjoyment by future generations of the national parks can be ensured only if the superb quality of park resources and values is left unimpaired, has provided that when there is a conflict between conserving resources and values and providing for enjoyment of them, conservation is to be predominant. This is how courts have consistently interpreted the Organic Act. | 1.4.3 [2001] The NPS Obligation to Conserve and Provide for Enjoyment of Park Resources and Values. The "fundamental purpose" of the national park system, established by the Organic Act and reaffirmed by the General Authorities Act, as amended, begins with a mandate to conserve park resources and values. This mandate is independent of the separate prohibition on impairment, and so applies all the time, with respect to all park resources and values, even when there is no risk that any park resources or values may be impaired. NPS managers must always seek ways to avoid, or to minimize to the greatest degree practicable, adverse impacts on park resources and values. However, the laws do give the Service the management discretion to allow impacts to park resources and values when necessary and appropriate to fulfill the purposes of a park, so long as the impact does not constitute impairment of the affected resources and values. The fundamental purpose of all parks also includes providing for the enjoyment of park resources and values by the people of the United States. The "enjoyment" that is contemplated by the statute is broad; it is the enjoyment of all the people of the United States, not just those who visit parks, and so includes enjoyment both by people who directly experience parks and by those who appreciate them from afar. It also includes deriving benefit (including scientific knowledge) and inspiration from parks, as well as other forms of enjoyment. Congress, recognizing that the enjoyment by future generations of the national parks can be ensured only if the superb quality of park resources and values is left unimpaired, has provided that when there is a conflict between conserving resources and values and providing for enjoyment of them, conservation is to be predominant. This is how courts have consistently interpreted the Organic Act, in decisions that variously describe it as making "resource protection the primary goal" or "resource protection the overarching concern," or as establishing a "primary mission of resource conservation," a "conservation mandate," "an overriding preservation mandate," "an overarching goal of resource protection," or "but a single purpose, namely, conservation." |
| 1.4.7 (2006) Decision-making Requirements to Identify and Avoid Impairments. Before approving a proposed action that could lead to an impairment of park resources and values, an NPS decisionmaker must consider the impacts of the proposed action and determine, in writing, that the activity will not lead to an impairment of park resources and values. If there would bean impairment, the action must not be approved. If it is determined that there is, or will be, an impairment, the decision-maker must take appropriate action, to the extent possible within the Service's authorities and available resources, to eliminate the impairment. The action must eliminate the impairment as soon as reasonably possible, taking into consideration the nature, duration, magnitude, and other characteristics of the impacts on park resources and values . . . . | 1.4.7 (2001) Decision-making Requirements to Avoid Impairments Before approving a proposed action that could lead to an impairment of park resources and values, an NPS decisionmaker must consider the impacts of the proposed action and determine, in writing, that the activity will not lead to an impairment of park resources and values. If there would be an impairment, the action may not be approved. In making a determination of whether there would be an impairment, a National Park Service decision-maker must use his or her professional judgment. The decision-maker must consider any environmental assessments or environmental impact statements required by the National Environmental Policy Act of 1969 (NEPA); relevant scientific studies, and other sources of information; and public comments. When an NPS decision-maker becomes aware that an ongoing activity might have led or might be leading to an impairment of park resources or values, he or she must investigate and determine if there is, or will be, an impairment. Whenever practicable, such an investigation and determination will be made as part of an appropriate park planning process undertaken for other purposes. If it determined that there is, or will be, such an impairment, the Director must take appropriate action, to the extent possible within the Service's authorities and available resources, to eliminate the impairment. The action must eliminate the impairment as soon as reasonably possible, taking into consideration the nature, duration, magnitude, and other characteristics of the impacts to park resources and values, as well as the requirements of NEPA, the Administrative Procedure Act, and other applicable law. |

Congress has no obligation to consider the President's recommendations, should he offer any, let alone act upon them. See Guerrero v. Clinton, 157 F.3d 1190, 1191 (9th Cir. 1998)(holding where "reports [to Congress] themselves trigger no legal consequences," any injury allegedly incurred by the absence of reporting "is . . . not redressable"). In short, the judicial order that TWS requests will not afford it the redress it seeks. At 10.

The court of appeals then turned to the *2001 Management Policies.* The Wilderness Society argued that NPS bound itself by the Policies to make timely wilderness reports to the president as well as to manage wilderness study areas in a manner consistent with wilderness preservation until Congress determined whether to include an area in the Wilderness System. The Justice Department, however, argued that the Guidelines were *not* binding, but rather simply advisory. The court of appeals concluded:

> The only ground offered by TWS [The Wilderness Society] to support its claim that NPS is legally obliged to provide management plans is § 6.3.4.2 of the MANAGEMENT POLICIES. The Government contends that the POLICIES does not embody rules that are enforceable against the agency; rather, according to the Government, the POLICIES provides only internal guidance for NPS managers and staff. We agree.

> TWS argues that the binding nature of the POLICIES was settled in Davis v. Latschar, 202 F.3d 359 (D.C. Cir. 2000). We are unconvinced. In Davis, the court accepted an "assertion" that NPS intended to be bound by the MANAGEMENT POLICIES, because the assertion was uncontested. The matter was not in dispute, so the court had no occasion to render a final judgment on the issue. The issue is squarely posed in this case, however, and the Government strenuously argues that the agency did not intend to establish binding rules when it promulgated the MANAGEMENT POLICIES. (Emphasis added.)

> In determining whether an agency has issued a binding norm or merely a statement of policy, we are guided by two lines of inquiry. "One line of analysis focuses on the effects of the agency action," asking whether the agency has "(1) impose[d] any rights and obligations," or (2) "genuinely [left] the agency and its decisionmakers free to exercise discretion." "[T]he language actually used by the agency" is often central to making such determinations. "The second line of analysis focuses on the agency's expressed intentions." The analysis under this line of cases "look[s] to three factors: (1) the [a]gency's own characterization of the action; (2) whether the action was published in the Federal Register or the Code of Federal Regulations; and (3) whether the action has binding effects on private parties or on the agency." (Internal citations omitted.)

Under either line of analysis, the MANAGEMENT POLICIES is a statement of policy, not a codification of binding rules. While the text of the POLICIES on occasion uses mandatory language, such as "will" and "must," the document as a whole does not read as a set of rules. It lacks precision in its directives, and there is no indication of how the enunciated policies are to be prioritized. It is particularly noteworthy that NPS did not issue its MANAGEMENT POLICIES through notice and comment rulemaking under 5 U.S.C. § 553 of the APA. Although the agency twice gave notice in the Federal Register of proposed policies, it never published a final version of the POLICIES in either the Federal Register or, more significantly, in the Code of Federal Regulations. Failure to publish in the Federal Register is indication that the statement in question was not meant to be a regulation since the [APA] requires regulations to be so published.

The converse, however, is not true: Publication in the Federal Register does not suggest that the matter published was meant to be a regulation, since the APA requires general statements of policy to be published as well. The real dividing point between regulations and general statements of policy is publication in the Code of Federal Regulations, which the statute authorizes to contain only documents "having general applicability and legal effect," and which the governing regulations provide shall contain current or future effect." The MANAGEMENT POLICIES never has been published in the Code of Federal Regulations. (Internal citations omitted.)

The agency's characterization of the MANAGEMENT POLICIES in the Federal Register is also telling. In its January 2000 announcement that a draft document was ready for public comment, the agency explained that [p]ark superintendents, planners, and other NPS employees use management policies as a reference source when making decisions that will affect units of the national park system." Notice of Availability of Draft National Park Service Management Policies, 65 Fed. Reg. 2984 (Jan. 19, 2000). This statement is consistent with the Introduction . . . :

Adherence to policy is mandatory unless specifically waived or modified in writing by the Secretary, the Assistant Secretary, or the Director. MANAGEMENT POLICIES, ...

This language does not evidence an intent on the part of the agency to limit its discretion and create enforceable rights. Rather, the agency's top administrators clearly reserved for themselves unlimited discretion to order and reorder all management priorities. <u>This supports the Government's contention that the POLICIES is no more than a set of internal guidelines for NPS managers and staff.</u> (Emphasis added.)

48

We find that, on the basis of the foregoing considerations, the conclusion is inescapable that the MANAGEMENT POLICES is a nonbinding, internal agency manual intended to guide and inform Park Service managers and staff. There is no indication that the agency meant for these internal directives to be judicially enforceable at the behest of members of the public who question the agency's management. For us to hold otherwise on this record would not only be contrary to our case law, but it would chill efforts by top agency officials to gain control over their bureaucratic charges through internal directives. In sum, the MANAGEMENT POLICIES is exactly what it appears to be, a guidance manual for NPS managers and staff that does not create enforceable regulations or modify existing legal rights. (Emphasis added.) At 19- 20.

The end result of this multi-year adventure is both curious and interesting. Considering all the fuss over the changes in policies, what is the real legal significance of the changes? Although NPS has policies, it now no longer wishes to be bound by those policies. In effect, the *2006 Management Policies* are simply advisory under the logic of the court of appeals decision in the Wilderness Society case and the disclaimer clause in the policy itself. This was not the agency's view of its management obligations in the 20th Century.

Looking at the situation from another perspective, one might say that national elections do have consequences![44] Certainly, future litigation over NPS legal roots will address this issue and further inform NPS of its responsibilities to manage the National Park System.

SALT CREEK REVISITED

NPS continued its quest to eliminate four-wheel-drive vehicles from Canyonlands. In August 2003, NPS proposed to amend 36 C.F.R. 7.44 to add Salt Creek above the Peekaboo Springs Campgrounds to the list of areas where motorized vehicles are prohibited. [68 F.R. 47527] This proposal was accompanied by a revised EA and the enthusiastic adoption of the rationale of the court of appeals decision in the SUWA case. The proposal also concluded that ORVs operating in Salt Creek would cause permanent impairment to a significant park resource. In 2001, the Fish and Wildlife Service also assisted the regulatory effort by declaring Salt Creek Canyon critical habitat for the threatened Mexican Spotted Owl. The Superintendent, accordingly, did an "about face" from the 1995 decision. What a difference a decade makes! The proposed rule was finalized on June 14, 2004, with an effective date of July 14, 2004. [69 F.R. 32871]

---

[44] Environmental groups may be hoping that after the 2008 election, the new administration will return NPS management policies to an enforceable standard, rather than just an advisory one, by removing the disclaimer clause.

The legal debate over the control of the Salt Creek trail and the application of R.S. 2477 continues. As previously noted, the State of Utah now claims in federal court a R.S. 2477 road right-of-way within the park. The Federal Register Notice characterizes this disagreement as follows:

> The EA/FONSI and the impairment finding with respect to motorized use of the Salt Creek trail were made as a direct result of the still-pending litigation brought by Southern Utah Wilderness Alliance challenging the permit system that Canyonlands instituted for motor vehicles to use this trail. Since this lawsuit was originally filed, State and local entities have asserted that the trail constitutes an R.S. 2477 right-of-way, which in this case would be a right-of-way across public lands in favor of the State and County. As noted previously, the NPS has concluded that the information available to it is not sufficient to demonstrate that a valid right-of-way was created prior to reservation of these lands and that closure to motorized vehicles is required to prevent an impermissible impairment to park resources. No evidence exists that either the State or County has ever managed or maintained this trail, nor have they commenced administrative or judicial proceedings to lead to a determination whether any such claims are valid. Nevertheless, should it be subsequently determined that the State and County do hold a valid R.S. 2477 right-of-way, the regulation will be revisited to ensure that it is consistent with the property rights that are afforded to the holders of such valid rights-of-way. At 32875

The outcome of this litigation may have a marginal effect on the new regulations for off-road-vehicles. NPS regulations related to resource protection could apply to a state-owned road within a park system area as long as those NPS regulations are more stringent than state law.

CONCLUSION

A decision to balance visitor use with protecting park resources at Canyonlands National Park ended up in the federal court system. The result was an expedited reevaluation of NPS management policies as they interpret the 1916 Organic Act and the 1978 Redwood Amendment, with two administrations and Congress seeking to put their footprints on the management of the National Park System.

The debate over NPS management policy may be eternal. The uncertainty over the enforceability of the *2006 Management Policies* ensures that this debate will continue for quite some time.

As Professor Winks so eloquently stated in his article ("The National Park Service Act of 1916: 'A Contradictory Mandate'?"), the meanings of words evolve over time. The vocabulary of 1916 had a different pitch than that of 2006. Because the English language is imprecise and the nuances of words slowly adjust, the meanings of "conservation," "impairment," and "visitor use" will continue to be controversial. When those words are applied on the ground in the day-to-day decisions of park managers, who must constantly balance these NPS legal mandates, debate is inevitable.

Another subtext involves political boundaries that exist to protect the resources of the National Park System for future generations. The park idea has captured the imagination of the American public that, once aroused, will not accept land management or political philosophies that threaten the cornerstone of park protection: "Unimpaired for future generations."

As the nation's principal conservation agency, the Department of the Interior has responsibility for most of our nationally owned public lands and natural resources. This includes fostering sound use of our land and water resources; protecting our fish, wildlife, and biological diversity; preserving the environmental and cultural values of our national parks and historical places; and providing for the enjoyment of life through outdoor recreation. The department assesses our energy and mineral resources and works to ensure that their development is in the best interests of all our people by encouraging stewardship and citizen participation in their care. The department also has a major responsibility for American Indian reservation communities and for people who live in island territories under U.S. administration.

NPS D-200   September 2008 / Printed on recycled paper.

www.ingramcontent.com/pod-product-compliance
Lightning Source LLC
Chambersburg PA
CBHW080549290526
45790CB00006B/2604